Reflections *from the*
Flock
Images of the Christian Life

Ken Johnson & Robert Tamasy

ACCENT BOOKS
Denver, Colorado

ACCENT BOOKS

A division of Accent Publications, Inc.
12100 West Sixth Avenue
P.O. Box 15337
Denver, Colorado 80215

Library of Congress Catalog Card Number 88-71116

ISBN 0-89636-219-1

CONTENTS

DEDICATION

To my beautiful wife, Ardie, whose life patterns all the lessons this book offers from her early childhood to the present.

She was a shepherdess in her youth, and her experiences woven into our family have been and are priceless. A dear partner and loving wife and mother—to her this book is dedicated with our prayers that many will benefit from its content.

Ken Johnson
February 1989

INTRODUCTION

Let's play word association for a moment. When you hear the word "sheep," what is the first thing that comes to mind? Little Bo Peep? The raw material for your favorite wool sweater? The lamb chop entree you enjoyed recently at your favorite restaurant? Or something to count when you're fighting your way through a sleepless night?

Because I had the opportunity to get to know some of them personally, I associate sheep with words such as "dumb," "helpless," and "misguided." But I also think of the many times sheep are referred to in a book called the Bible, usually as an analogy to people. How can that be? People aren't dumb, or helpless, or misguided—or are they?

The Bible offers some interesting observations on that count. For instance, in the Old Testament book of Isaiah, it is written that, "All of us like sheep have gone astray, each of us has turned to his own way..." (Isaiah 53:6). But why the comparison to sheep? Why not owls or horses or lions? For years I accepted the biblical analogy of people and sheep in a general sense. Even though at times I asked the same questions, those references did not seem to have any practical meaning for me.

Then one day I began raising sheep as a hobby. I had the opportunity to observe those woolly animals closely, sometimes eye to eye. Although I really did not know what to expect when I began my adventures with sheep, I later discovered my fourteen years of feeding, protecting, and caring for lambs, ewes, and rams had given me a wealth of spiritual insights.

In reading the Bible, it seems clear that God is fond of comparing mankind, his foremost creation ("created in His own image" Genesis 1:27), to those funny creatures that wear their wool lining on the outside. The word sheep appears more than 120 times in the Bible. Add the words shepherd, lambs, flock, and fold, and you find that total reaches well into the hundreds.

It can be somewhat annoying to think of God equating us to sheep. A friend once commented about a church he usually passed each morning while driving to work. It was called the Church of the Good Shepherd. This businessman, a new Christian, admitted that he was bothered by that name. "That would mean, then, that I am a sheep. I really don't like that association," he said. "Sheep are pretty dumb animals, aren't they?"

He was right. Sheep certainly do demonstrate a lack of intelligence at times, perhaps more than most other animals. When God distributed common sense and mental capacity to His many creatures, for some reason He decided to be stingy with the sheep. However, after the years of tending my own sheep in a variety of circumstances, and although humans are the most intelligent living things on earth, I am convinced that God still has us pegged correctly in His book. In fact, there are times when we are so much like sheep it is disturbing.

I don't claim to be the world's foremost authority on sheep and their idiosyncracies. I'm a businessman by profession and have spent most of my working career managing people. Until recently, when I moved and sold the last of my sheep, I was just a part-time shepherd. (The word "part-time" is somewhat of a misnomer, however, since sheep have a way of eliciting more of your attention than you intend to give them.) It was my custom to go directly from my little flock of sheep to my office at the telephone company, or vice versa, making me a sort of shepherd in a three-piece suit.

What amazed me was how often my experiences with sheep seemed to have direct application to various areas of my life. I frequently saw a practical value for these lessons in business as I worked with both people and projects. There was ample relevance, as well, to my family life, community activities, and even church participation. As I shared some of these observations, I discovered that they are equally valid for custodians and corporate executives, airline pilots and athletes, heart specialists and homemakers, politicians and police officers.

For example, soon after I began taking care of sheep, I realized a little known fact about Bo Peep: She was wrong! You cannot leave sheep alone to fend for themselves—at least not for very long. If you do, your chances of keeping sheep are not very good. They need continual care and attention. Obviously, the same principle is true in business and with the family. You have to stay in contact with your employees and their needs; it is even more important with your spouse and children. Without that regular interaction, difficult and sometimes insurmountable problems can arise with surprising speed.

It may be that when God created sheep, His primary intent was to provide His human creations with handy object lessons so we could understand ourselves better. Perhaps he chose to add the benefits of wool and the tastiness of lamb chops as a bonus—reasons for us to keep sheep near enough to observe their behavior. I think we are fortunate that we usually cannot see ourselves as the Lord sees us. If we did, I suspect that when we talked to Him in prayer, we would do so much more sheepishly.

In the following chapters, I want to share some of my experiences in raising sheep, along with some observations. Read them and reach your own conclusion to the question: Are we really like sheep? I believe that if we can gain a better understanding of what God can teach us through these simple but lovable animals, it can help equip us to be of greater service to Him. I hope these insights will be as meaningful to you as they have been for me and my family.

"It is He who has made us, and not we ourselves; we are His people and the sheep of His pasture" (Psalm 100:3).

—Ken Johnson

Reflections from the Flock

Flock

Images of the Christian Life

CHAPTER ONE

SPECIAL DELIVERY

"He said to him, 'Tend My Lambs'..."
—John 21:15—

As I settled into the driver's seat of my car and closed the door, I felt the tension begin to ease. It had been a hectic day of meetings, wrestling with problems, and making decisions. A typical day. When someone picks up a telephone to make a call, he expects the instrument to function properly and complete the call quickly. It was my job at Northwestern Bell—and that of the people working under me—to meet those expectations. Few things, I discovered, could incite a normal human being's wrath faster than a malfunctioning telephone.

On this particular day, I felt I had more than earned my pay after dealing with a seeming multitude of problems. I looked forward to getting home. The thirty minute drive from St. Paul to rural Lake Elmo would give me time to unwind and mentally change hats—from businessman to family man.

It was early spring, and I enjoyed the final moments of daylight, even though it was grey and overcast, since I had spent most of the day with nothing more appealing to look at than plain office walls. Warmth had not yet returned to the frozen frontier we know as Minnesota. Winter's brisk bite continued to hold fast, as did the layer of frosty white which coated the countryside. Fortunately, my calendar reassured me the land would soon undergo a rebirth. Since there was no visible evidence, I accepted that on faith. (I believe spring is appreciated nowhere as much as in Minnesota, since the season arrives after so many months of icy bondage.)

My family and I enjoyed Lake Elmo. It was close enough to the city for convenience, but far enough to allow us to escape the hubbub of urban living. For me, it was a pleasant contrast—work in the city and private life in the country.

A few miles from home, I remembered that this would not be a normal evening in the Johnson household. In retrospect, that may have been one of the greatest understatements of my life.

My wife, Ardie, was 100 miles away, visiting her mother in Sandstone, Minnesota. That was not unusual, since after our children became old enough to care for themselves for an hour or so until I got home, she occasionally would make a brief visit north. However, that meant for tonight my hats would be those of both dad and mom.

Quickly I began running down my mental checklist: What should I fix for supper? I wonder if the kids will need me to help with their homework? Let's see, tonight's Wednesday, right? That means we'll have to be ready for church by 7:15.

I also remembered our small flock of sheep. Although we weren't vocational farmers, we had started raising sheep as a pleasant "pastime." It was lambing season, and our ewes were due to deliver soon. "I wonder how they're doing?" I asked myself. Although I didn't realize it then, that question would force other, more mundane concerns such as supper and homework quickly into the background.

We lived on a 24-acre farm, and since our house was about 150 feet off the road, it sat hidden behind the trees as someone approached. I suppose that's why our big, weather-beaten mailbox at the front of the driveway always seemed like a "welcome home" sign to me. It was a friendly sight, especially after a demanding workday, even though there were times when I wished an incinerator were attached to the back of it for things like junk mail, circulars, and bills.

On this night, the mailbox was not alone. My eight-year-old son, Jim, was waiting for me also. Instantly, I thought, "Something's up." I suspected my plans for the evening were about to be reshuffled.

In the few moments before I reached the driveway, I reviewed the possibilities: Was there a problem at school? Maybe Jim's report card wasn't very good? Could the furnace have gone out? (On March days in Minnesota, thermal underwear is still recommended attire.) Maybe there was an important message from Ardie? Or could it be a news bulletin from the sheep nursery?

Jim was obviously agitated. On a scale of one to ten, his expressions of emotion usually rate around a two or three, but as I stopped the car and rolled down the window, I saw he was about to jump out of his snowboots with excitement.

Frantically, he tried to blurt out his assessment of the problem. Some people write in shorthand; my son was talking to me in "short-speak." The words came

15

pouring out too fast for me to understand, so finally I asked him to stop, take a breath, and start over. "Tell me again, slower. What's our problem?"

"There's a head sticking out of one of the ewes!" he exclaimed.

That is the normal way for a lamb to be born, but Jim explained the lamb had been in that position for some time, and its mother seemed to be having difficulty. Although I didn't have a B.S. (bachelor of shepherding), and had only begun raising sheep a few years earlier, the situation didn't sound right. Usually, once a lamb pokes its head out of the womb, birth is just seconds away.

I told Jim to jump into the car. We drove up to the house and immediately trudged over to the barn. I knew the ewe would not notice whether her shepherd was wearing a three-piece suit or overalls. As we neared the barn, I could tell that my son was right. I heard a low moaning coming from the ewe indicating that she was in considerable distress.

As we entered the barn, I saw the ewe lying on her side. Judging from the straw, dirt, and other matter stuck in her woolly coat, I realized she had been rolling in agony on the floor. The lamb's tiny, moist head also was covered with the debris, eyes closed, and it wasn't an appealing sight. I did not know for certain, but my initial thought was, "There is one dead lamb."

> Something had to be
> done, but I wasn't
> sure what!

Analyzing the situation, I was not overcome by great

waves of optimism. I knew something had to be done, but I was unsure what. We hurried back to the house so I could change into clothes more suited for whatever I needed to do. A dark grey suit and vest may be the way to dress for success in business, but it's definitely out of style at a lamb birthing.

To be honest, I doubted that we could be of much help to the unfortunate ewe and her new offspring. I did know that if we were to succeed, it would take more than my urban-oriented ingenuity. For a veteran sheepherder, this might have been a routine situation; for me it was a major crisis. After all, I was a telephone company department manager. Raising sheep was just my avocation—or so I had thought.

I have long advocated the motto, "When in doubt, pray," so I did—out loud. "Lord, we're really going to need your help in this one. I know that is one of your creatures out there struggling to get into this world, so I'd appreciate your wisdom in what we should do."

While I was changing clothes, I evaluated my options. If Ardie had been home, I could have counted on her for advice. As a girl, she had grown up on a farm and had helped in raising her family's sheep. She also was a registered nurse, which would have come in handy. Jim, apparently thinking along the same lines, suggested, "Let's call Mom." I pointed out she was too far away to be of any assistance.

My next door neighbor was the local authority on sheep, having raised them for quite a few years. In fact, he had gotten us started with the animals, so I dialed his phone number. There is one shortcoming of telephones, even when they are working right. They aren't much good if the person you want to talk with is not home. When my neighbor failed to answer his phone, I knew I couldn't count on his help either.

"Well, Jim," I said, "We've got to give it a try and see if we can help the ewe." We called my 12-year-old daughter, Janelle, from her room and told her we needed her assistance. She had just settled down to do her homework, and I could tell by her less than enthusiastic response that she wasn't excited about going back into the cold to help some "dumb old sheep." But at our insistence, she bundled up and joined us as we started back through the snow to the barn.

When we got there, the ewe's dilemma had not improved. She appeared even more exhausted from the additional time that had elapsed. Squatting down to inspect more closely, I understood the problem. Normally, a lamb is born with its front feet and forelegs coming out at the same time as the head. In this case, the forelegs had remained behind the head, and a shoulder was preventing the lamb from sliding down the ewe's birth canal. Clearly, the lamb was not going to work itself out. I knew my only course of action was to try pulling it out.

I also knew that would not be as simple as is sounded. For one thing, I have very large hands. It would not be easy to slip my hand into that small opening—particularly with a lamb already blocking the way. Yet, it was our only recourse. In business there are times when you do the unorthodox to solve a problem, and this was a similar situation. Big paws or not, I resolved to try working my hand inside the ewe and somehow maneuver the lamb's shoulder around to pull it out.

At times the unorthodox is required to solve a problem

I asked Janelle to hold the ewe steady; the weakened sheep did not resist my daughter's firm grasp. Meanwhile, Jim did the best thing he could think of— he went to a corner of the barn, knelt, and started to pray. I smiled as he put his faith into practice; his idea seemed to be the best of all. I said another silent prayer, then began trying to ease my hand inside the mother sheep. For some reason, the old television show "Mission: Impossible" flashed through my mind.

With Janelle maintaining her grip on the sheep, I thrust in my hand as hard and as far as I could, desperately trying to grasp the lamb's leg. As I did this, I became convinced the lamb was dead, but I knew the ewe's life was in jeopardy also. My efforts seemed futile. I was in an awkward position, and I couldn't get enough leverage to free the lamb's foreleg and bring it out.

I was about to give up when I noticed Jim out of the corner of my eye. I was impressed by how intently he was praying. Every so often he would pause to ask, "How's it going, Dad?" and then return to his prayerful posture.

Even Janelle was caught up in the excitement and suspense of the moment. Her unfinished homework lay in the house, forgotten. Her independent spirit had been set aside temporarily as we worked together as a team—she bracing the ewe, Jim serving as our prayer warrior, and me persistently pushing and pulling.

I gave one additional thrust with my arm; suddenly, I had a grip on one leg. I worked the leg out of the womb alongside the head and within seconds the lamb slid out as cleanly and easily as if there never had been a problem.

The lamb lay there on the barn floor, showing no sign of life. Just in case, I gave it a tap on the side—and it coughed! We (and even the ewe, I believe) gave a sigh of relief. In spite of her travail, the sheep quickly began her motherly chores. We watched the amazing scene for a minute, exchanging happy smiles. Confident that we had done all we could do, I herded Jim and Janelle toward the house.

"Kids, let's leave her alone with the lamb." I knew the ewe would be able to complete the remaining details. Watching the mother clean up the lamb and get it moving would have been an anticlimax to the miracle in which we had just participated.

We, too, had to get cleaned up. If we hurried, there still was enough time to change clothes, eat, and drive to church. I was thankful Ardie had prepared some meals in advance, and we merely had to warm up our supper.

In less than thirty minutes we were ready. Before leaving, we decided to check to see how the ewe and her newborn were getting along. To our surprise, the miracle had taken on even greater significance: In that brief span of time, the ewe had borne a second lamb! In this case there had been no complications, and we rejoiced over having taken part in the birth of twin lambs.

It was a special moment in our lives. I had survived my first attempt as a sheep midwife, and the wonder of birth had been impressed indelibly upon each of us.

We had succeeded without the help of the "pros"—
Ardie, my neighbor, or the veterinarian. God's help had
been sufficient. My son's prayers had been answered so
clearly. In the years since, that experience has
confirmed for both Jim and Janelle their belief in the
God who created all we see and touch. They also have
greater appreciation for the gift of life.

> You just do what you
> think is right, as
> well as you can

It also gave us a good lesson in perseverence.
Sometimes in life there is no choice of alternatives. You
just do what you think is right, as well as you can. It
would have been easy to give up, resigning ourselves to
the apparent hopelessness of freeing the lamb from its
mother's womb. Fortunately we didn't, since it would
have cost three lives—the ewe and her twins.

Incidents like this were not the norm during the
fourteen years I shepherded a flock of about twenty
sheep. But there was an endless variety of problems.
Although few were as urgent as the lamb stuck in limbo
during labor, each experience made a lasting impression. As I cared for these lovable, but generally helpless
creatures, it was fascinating to discover that in many
respects, we are not unlike sheep.

In the Bible, the sheep theme recurs throughout the
Old and New Testaments. For example, in the book of
Ezekiel, it is written, "For thus says the Lord God,
'Behold, I Myself will search for My sheep and seek
them out. As a shepherd cares for his herd in the day
when he is among his scattered sheep, so I will care for

p and will deliver them from all the places to ...hey were scattered on a cloudy and gloomy (34:11-12). Looking back, I can identify with the idea of delivering sheep on a cloudy and gloomy day!

I had been reading the Bible for a number of years before I encountered sheep "up close and personal." It was exciting to see the Scriptures come alive in my daily dealings with those mild-mannered mammals. To my surprise, the principles I learned among the sheep also applied to other areas of my life. There was another time when prayer and teamwork helped to give birth—in this instance, to a new idea.

In 1970, my managerial responsibilities were simple: All I had to do was see that commercial and residential telephone service was maintained without disruption. It was another mission impossible. That year Northwestern Bell was plagued by a lot of aging, tired equipment. It seemed there was always something breaking down. Phone service generally was taken for granted by our customers, except when they lost it unexpectedly. On such occasions, they would go to amazing lengths to express that assumption, making clear their desire to resume normal use of their telephones.

Because of the heavy volume of repair work we were doing, it seemed logical to me to hire a dispatcher to coordinate the response of repair crews to trouble areas. Up to that time, our trouble analyzers also coordinated repair assignments. The result was a disjointed, inefficient operation. Too often, our repair crews crisscrossed in responding to calls around the city. This created additional delays before disrupted service could be restored.

A full-time dispatcher was a new concept, and I knew the proposal would require careful presentation to receive union support. I felt this job could be handled readily by a woman, and I knew that was another potential obstacle to adopting my plan. The women's movement was still years away at that time, and the union aggressively sought to preserve jobs as they were, which included not giving new work to women. Men working on the outside also would resist a plan calling for them to take orders from a woman dispatcher. I was convinced the idea needed to be implemented, but I was concerned about disrupting employee/employer relations.

As my idea took form, I determined the dispatching of repair crews could be coordinated by using an electronic display board with multiple sets of red and green lights controlled from one panel. The dispatcher would pinpoint trouble areas on the map, turn on a red light on the board for that part of the city, and wait until the nearest repairmen became available. Red would mean there was trouble in an area with no available repairmen. Green would indicate there was trouble, but a repair crew was on the scene. The plan seemed simple enough; if only the workers would accept it.

My first step was to pray about the problem. I asked God to give me wisdom in how to communicate the situation and the proposed remedy. Then, I explained the idea to my staff. I wanted to involve them in the solution and solicited their suggestions on how to do it. One crew member, who enjoyed carpentry as a hobby, offered to build the display board. Another technician, whose pastime was electronics, volunteered to do the wiring for the board. Several other men also were able to contribute to the project in various ways.

In the end, we all helped in developing an efficient new method for dispatching our repair crews. We selected one of the top women clerks in the office to serve as the dispatcher.

The day we turned on the new system, everything went smoothly. There were times when outside servicemen complained about the dispatching method, but union leaders defended the project since they had been involved in its development. This system later was written up in a prominent trade journal, and at least one railroad line adapted our display board for its uses.

Being a manager, a husband, or a father is very much like being a shepherd. You have to demonstrate sincere concern for your "sheep," and it is important to demonstrate that you are trustworthy. Once that is established, it's not hard to be a leader.

THOUGHTS TO CONSIDER AND DISCUSS:

1. Who are the "lambs" in your life for whom you are responsible? (John 21:15)

2. Think of a time when your "circuits" at work or in your home seemed like they were going into overload. Did you feel you were asked to do more than you were able to handle? How did you cope with the situation? (Consider Philippians 4:13.)

3. What is the role of prayer in your life? In a crisis, why do we look on prayer as our "last resort"? How do you feel I Thessalonians 5:17 relates to you?

CHAPTER TWO

DON'T FENCE ME IN

"Then the lambs will graze as in their pasture..."
—Isaiah 5:17—

My introduction to sheep-raising was not the realization of a lifelong dream. It happened, as a matter of fact, almost by accident.

Ardie had grown up on a farm, but endured a separation from the rural lifestyle she loved after we got married. After being transferred from one city to another in Minnesota, when we had an opportunity to move to the Minneapolis/St. Paul area, Ardie made only one stipulation: She wanted us to find a house in the country, away from the city. I suppose you can take the farm girl off the farm but you can't get the farm out of the farm girl.

When I accepted my new assignment with Northwestern Bell, we began looking for our rural home. Soon we found a farm that pleased us both. The only problem was that it consisted of forty acres, and we could not afford to buy that much property. When we told the real estate agent, he asked how many acres we thought we could afford. His question seemed unusual. We knew it is generally easier for a realtor to sell a

25

parcel of land in one piece rather than breaking it into smaller tracts with possibly less buyer appeal. However, with his help, we worked out an arrangement to buy twenty-four acres. Suddenly, we had a farm.

The next question was, what should we do with it? At first we planned a large garden and thought it would be nice to get some animals for our children, perhaps for a 4-H project. We did have one animal, a horse, which came with the farm. He seemed like a nice horse, but having spent little time around horses, I knew virtually nothing about them. If you had asked me what kind of horse he was, I would have replied, "A brown one." I learned later that it was an Arabian.

Since we wanted to live in some degree of harmony with our neighbors, we determined that grazing animals would help to keep the grass and weeds at a respectable height. Pigs were the first animals we tried, but they quickly discouraged us. They were very destructive, breaking windows and doors in the barn. Also, they weren't slowed very much by the fences we had. It was hard to catch them, and a dirty task to feed them.

Eventually we got rid of the four pigs—all females— by selling them to my brother-in-law, Howard. He also had a farm and was more experienced in raising pigs, so we felt it was a good trade off. Over the next few years our reject hogs proved to be a tremendous investment for Howard since they presented him with more than $10,000 in baby pigs.

Next we experimented with chickens, but they proved to be more trouble than they were worth. Feeding costs were high, and they didn't have much appeal for our children. Did you ever try to hug a chicken?

In this case, we did have more experience. Ardie had helped raise chickens when she was a girl, but had not always been successful. She vividly remembers the first time she tried to kill a chicken for dinner. Her mother usually performed that task, and following her example, Ardie attempted to coax the chicken to lay its neck across a log. Holding the chicken with one hand, she raised the ax, swung. . .and cut off the bird's beak! I understand the chicken never clucked the same after that.

The weather was really responsible for our introduction to sheep. It was during our third summer at the farm, and it had hardly rained for weeks. Because of the drought, grass in the pastures was growing very slowly. After animals had grazed on some acreage for awhile, it was used up for the season. It then became necessary to move them to a new section of pasture.

Toward the end of the summer, our neighbor to the east had run out of pasture land for his sheep, so he asked if he could use some of our land. Our pastures weren't being used, so we were happy to oblige him. We thought nothing more about it, but as the summer ended, the neighbor felt he owed us something to compensate for use of our land. The "payment" came in the form of several lambs. Since we were still undecided about what kind of animals to raise, we accepted them.

Thus we became the owners of several fuzzy, cuddly little sheep. I didn't know much about sheep then, but Ardie did, again calling upon her girlhood experiences on the farm. She was delighted to have the lambs.

I never could have guessed how much I would learn from our sheep over the next fourteen years. The first thing I discovered was how enjoyable they were to have around. Compared to our pigs, who had behaved most of the time like naughty teenagers, the sheep acted like innocent babies, totally dependent and appreciative of everything that was done for them. Even then I could begin to see similarities between sheep and people.

The grass seemed greener that hot, dry summer

The seasons passed. It was another hot, dry summer—much like when we first got our lambs. By the end of the summer, blades of grass in our pasture were as scarce as five-leaf clover. The sheep, of course, did not understand. They just knew they were hungry and wanted to eat.

We decided a temporary alternative was to let the sheep feed on the grass in our side yard, which amounted to nearly an acre. We realized that a landscape specialist passing by might suffer cardiac arrest, but aesthetics had to be secondary to the well-being of our sheep.

To do that, we had to erect a temporary fence to keep the sheep contained and prevent them from eating the flowers and shrubs Ardie had so carefully cultivated. Even though the fence would be only an interim part of our lawn decor, we made sure it was firmly in place before bringing in our twenty sheep. Sheep have an annoying habit of pushing or bumping into fences, so any barrier, permanent or short-term, could not be haphazardly erected.

It took several hours to put up the four-foot fence of seven woven-wire strands interwoven with vertical strands strung horizontally from posts. The rectangular holes were smallest at the bottom, to prevent lambs from sneaking through, and wider at the top since even adult sheep cannot climb through at that height.

When the job was completed, we let the sheep into the fresh, new pasture area, never before touched by lambish limbs. As we opened the gate, the sheep romped in excitedly and began inspecting the new surroundings. Soon they were busily chomping on the new grass, quickly forgetting that they had just entered territory previously uncharted for them. Meanwhile, I and my family retreated to the house to reward our hard labors with a hearty lunch. Less than fifteen minutes later I happened to glance out the window at an amazing scene.

Across the yard, lined up tightly along the new fence, stood each of the twenty sheep. Each one's head was through the fence strands, and they were pushing and straining against the fence to reach the blades of grass farthest from them. I was thankful that the fence was sturdy, because the muscles in the rear legs of each animal were tensed with the exertion of trying to reach what lay on the other side of the boundary.

Our woolly friends still had plenty of grass to eat on their side of the fence, but apparently the grass on the opposite side looked greener and more appealing. It was amazing how a simple fence could make identical sections of grass look so different! None of the sheep paused to consider if it might be easier—and less strenuous—to eat the grass beneath their feet.

Watching our sheep, so intent upon attaining the unattainable, I realized that the adage, "The grass is always greener on the other side of the fence," did not originate in the mind of some literary immortal. It probably had its roots in the observations of some wise, old shepherd who had grown to know his flocks well over the years. I also couldn't help reflecting on how we, like the sheep, contend with our own personal fences, determined to get to the "greener grass" on the other side. Unfortunately, most of the time the alluring "grass" is neither brighter nor a richer shade of green; it just appears that way from a distance.

We never know when
the "syndrome" will
strike next

Have you ever been victimized by the "grass is greener syndrome"? I suspect all of us have at one time or another. Maybe it's on the job, wishing we worked for another company or that we had a more understanding boss like someone else we know. Perhaps we wonder why our marriage doesn't seem nearly as exciting as that of the attractive couple at church, or why our children are not as well-behaved as the youngsters across the street. Sometimes it appears that everyone else drives a Rolls, while our car hardly rolls at all!

A few years ago, Ardie and I were reminded that the grass may seem greener concerning even relatively unimportant things. After moving from our native Minnesota to Tennessee in 1983, we were excited by the prospect of enjoying warm weather for longer periods of time. In particular, we thought how great it would be to barbecue many of our meals on an outdoor grill. As we pondered the grill of our dreams, we decided our old, black-domed charcoal model would not be satisfactory. What we needed for barbecue perfection was a propane-fueled gas grill! I imagined the difference we would taste in our steaks, chickens, hamburgers, and hot dogs, although I did have mixed feelings about lamb chops.

One day we commented to a neighbor about our interest in a gas grill. "That's a coincidence," she replied. "I have two grills. One is propane and the other is natural gas. I've been thinking about trying one of those black-domed, charcoal grills." To her, the grass on our side of the fence looked greener, too!

There is an interesting thing that happens when sheep begin pushing against a fence to reach the grass on the opposite side. Their straining usually ruins the grass right beneath their feet, more grass than they could ever hope to reach on the other side. If sheep could analyze their actions, they would realize how foolish and greedy they are. However, they never stop to evaluate. They just proceed stubbornly with blind determination, following their impulses.

I wish sheep were alone in that characteristic, but, in fact, sometimes people aren't much different. I've known some human "sheep" who responded in the same way, ruining some precious "turf" in the process. For example, years ago I knew a successful professional man who had a lovely family. He didn't seem to lack anything. He had a beautiful home, cars, nice clothes, respect in the community. For a number of months we met regularly for breakfast or lunch to discuss common interests and became fairly good friends.

This man seemed to have a good perspective on life. He seemed to understand the perils of excessive pride and the endless pursuit of personal gain, but in time, it became evident that he was a fence straddler. Despite all he had on his own side of the fence, he continued to gaze longingly toward the enticing "greener grass" on the other side.

He began to give in to the lures of wealth, prestige, and self-gratification. Although wealth is not necessarily wrong in itself, this man clearly was afflicted by what the Bible terms, "the love of money." Despite his prospering career, my friend felt a compelling desire to diversify into other businesses. He started by investing in a venture totally unrelated to his profession, and then eagerly grabbed an opportunity to do consulting work.

His personal tastes began to change, and material possessions became increasingly important. Our friendship was weakened by the growing conflict between what we viewed as the significant things in life. I was saddened, because it was evident that the change in my friend was not for the better.

Eventually, the greener grass expanded beyond business pursuits and acquiring more "things." He became intimately involved with another woman, resulting in the disintegration of his marriage, the loss of his wife and his children's adoration. The other woman? In time she faded from the scene. Many of his business investments turned sour, resulting in financial difficulty. A once promising life encountered terrible tragedy, and it was all so unnecessary. When I remember this man, it occurs to me he was not so different from my silly sheep, with their heads pushed through a temporary fence.

In our society, one of the greatest perpetrators of the greener grass myth is television. I enjoy watching TV from time to time, but it seems many of the commercials and much of the programming is geared toward tantalizing us with what we don't have, rather than encouraging us to appreciate what we do have. Sometimes after watching television for awhile, it's hard to distinguish "wants" from "needs." Whether it is a wonderful new shampoo or the latest, most sophisticated automobile, TV seems to constantly tease us: "Don't you think the grass is greener on this other side?"

There's more than one side to a fence

Interestingly, this fence issue has another side—no pun intended. Although fences serve to restrict our access to what surrounds us, they can provide security and a sense of peace also.

Whenever our sheep were turned out to an unfamiliar area, they became skittish. They were fearful of the slightest commotion, and usually stood in one place until they located the fence. Once they had determined their new borders, they would settle down and resume their normal routine. One part of their nature challenged them to reach for what they saw beyond the fence, but another part appreciated the protection of the fence. Disturbances outside the fence did not disrupt their tranquility as long as all remained calm within their boundaries.

I've discovered this same principle applies to the family. One reason children disobey, experts tell us, is to test their boundaries. It's not that they resent the boundaries, they just want to clarify where they are so they can operate freely within those limits. My youngest daughter, Jolene, is particularly adept at that!

Dr. James Dobson, the prominent authority on the family, writes in his book *Dr. Dobson Answers Your Questions:*

> *When a child behaves in ways that are disrespectful or harmful to himself or others, his hidden purpose is often to verify the stability of the boundaries. . .a child who assaults the loving authority of his parents is greatly reassured when their leadership holds firm and confident. He finds his greatest security in a structured environment where the rights of other people (and his own) are protected by definite boundaries.* [1]

In one sense, the husband and wife relationship works in a similar way. Several times Ardie has told me, "I want to know where my fences are." She wants to know my expectations for her, such as how much money she can spend without needing to consult with me first. Once she has that framework, she knows she can carry out her responsibilities for the home and our children without causing a conflict with me. And as a husband/father who is called by God to provide leadership in our home, I'm shirking my responsibilities if I fail to offer those guidelines.

The same is true in the workplace. An employee works most effectively when he clearly understands his job responsibilities, has been informed of his employer's expectations, and knows the limitations within which he is asked to perform.

In Isaiah 53:6, the prophet wrote, "All of us like sheep have gone astray." We have fought against our fences and sometimes grabbed for greener grass. In most cases we discover that our vision has been colored by the lures of worldliness, materialism, power, prestige, and pride. At the same time, we have valued our fences. We don't want them taken down; we just like to test them from time to time. Sometimes our fences are our greatest weapon against anxiety and insecurity.

THOUGHTS TO CONSIDER AND DISCUSS:

1. Recall an experience—a possible job change, a different home, a new car, etc.—when the "grass seemed greener" elsewhere, but you later discovered your own "pasture" was as good or better. What made the alternative so appealing at the time?

2. Is there an area of "greener grass" in your life now? How can you best evaluate your choices? What part does honoring God have in your considerations? How can Matthew 6:33 assist us in decision making?

3. What brings security into your life? What things seem to threaten that security? How can we find stable, secure lives in a world filled with uncertainty and insecurity? (Isaiah 41:10)

FOOTNOTES

[1] *Dr. Dobson Answers Your Questions* by James Dobson © 1982, Word Books, Waco, Texas, p. 120.

CHAPTER THREE

LET'S PLAY FOLLOW THE LEADER

"The Lord is my shepherd. . .He leads me beside quiet waters."
—Psalm 23:1-2—

One chilly morning the alarm clock roused me out of my wintry hibernation. With the determination of a fullback fighting for the final yard into the end zone, I pushed myself out of bed to greet another day. With the nip in the air, I briefly entertained a thought to crawl back under the covers, but thinking of the busy day ahead convinced me I needed to move into action.

After showering and shaving, I slid into my coveralls and headed for the barn to tend to the sheep. As I opened the barn door and called to them, I grabbed a hoe to do a quick cleanup just outside the door. I could hear the sleepy sheep moving about, beginning to shuffle toward the doorway.

Acting on a playful impulse, I took the hoe handle and held it in front of the first ewe, about knee high, as she started out the door. Instead of stopping, she gracefully leaped over the stick and proceeded, without hesitation, toward the pasture.

I pulled the hoe handle away, but was fascinated to see what happened next. One after another, each of the remaining twenty sheep came to where the first ewe had jumped—and duplicated the feat! As if on command, each sheep launched itself into the air at that precise spot, completed its jump, and then fell in step with the animal directly in front of it.

What a curious sight! The fact that the original reason for jumping—the hoe handle—had been taken away did not seem to concern the little flock of sheep at all. All they knew was that the sheep immediately in front had jumped, and that seemed to be reason enough for doing the same.

That was years ago, but I can still picture those silly sheep following one another's lead unquestioningly. It reminded me of a game we used to play when I was a boy, "Follow the Leader." Perhaps you played it, too. The rules were simple: The leader performed a series of stunts, and we repeated them, one by one. They may have included parading along the sidewalk, going up and down stairways, jumping, running, walking, even crawling. In this game, however, we followed the leader because we wanted to.

We've always done it that way before

As adults, there are times when we still seem to be playing that game, even though we may not be aware of it. I saw this illustrated at a service club luncheon I attended not long ago. The meeting began at noon, which does not seem particularly unusual, except this club had begun its luncheons at 12:10 p.m. for as long as anyone could remember. The new club president—a real troublemaker—had immediately questioned the starting time, since most other local clubs began their activities at noon. No one could explain why theirs began at ten minutes after noon. The only answer anyone had was, "Well, we've always done it that way." When the president suggested changing the club's meeting time to 12 noon, no one objected. A few members wondered why it had not been done sooner. (Now if we can only figure out why 12 o'clock is generally accepted as the official lunch hour!)

I'm reminded of a man whose wife suffered from a classic example of "follow the leader" syndrome. It seems that whenever she prepared a ham for dinner, she had an unusual habit of cutting off both ends of the ham before putting it into the oven. There may be a good reason for doing that, he thought, but it seems like a waste of good meat. Finally, he asked, "Honey, why do you cut the ends off the ham and throw them away?"

"That's the way Mother always cooked our hams when I was growing up," his wife responded.

Her answer seemed reasonable, but it failed to answer the question, "Why?" The next time he saw his mother-in-law, the husband could hardly wait to ask, "Mom, Lil always cuts both ends off our hams before she puts them in to cook. She says she learned that from you. I was just wondering—why do you do it?" The mother-in-law replied, "That is the way my mother cooked her hams when I was growing up."

Fortunately, Grandma was still living, so the investigation did not end there. At the next family gathering, the curious husband was eager to pose his question again. "Grandma, Lil always cuts off both ends of the ham before putting it in to cook. She learned it from her mom, and her mom says she learned if from you. Why did you do it?"

With her eyes sparkling, Grandma smiled and leaned toward her grandson-in-law, as if to share a secret of the ages. "You see, in our home I had just one little cooking pan, and the only way I could fit a ham into it was to cut off both ends first!"

In business, "follow the leader" can present real problems. You've probably been in a situation like this: A veteran manager leaves the company after a number of years and a new boss arrives, filled with new ideas and innovations. Almost immediately, he encounters resistance. "Well, Mr. Smith never did it that way. Would you like me to show you how he used to do it?"

Our age of rapidly advancing technology is particularly troublesome for those who like the comfort of old ways. A new bookkeeping or records-keeping system may offer much greater speed and efficiency, but frequently our first reaction is a lack of confidence. "The old way has served us long and faithfully. It still works. Why reinvent the wheel?" we say (at least to ourselves).

We also follow the leader in other ways. I've lost count of how many times I went to the end of a long line in a bank or grocery store, only to discover moments later that a teller or cashier was waiting on the opposite side without any customers. If you pass someone on the street who is looking straight up, aren't you tempted to look up, too?

Modern-day advertising is firmly rooted in "follow the leader" psychology. Every day well-known celebrities appear on TV and radio, telling us that he or she uses a specific kind of toothpaste or shampoo, or wears a special line of clothing. Soon we are flocking to the stores to buy that certain product, simply because the famous "leader" says it is good.

I have to admit following the leader has sometimes been embarrassing for me. There was the time, for example, when I was led astray—not by a flock of sheep—but by a herd of cows! While Ardie and I were dating, I sometimes would go with her to her parents' farm in Sandstone, Minnesota. By this time, the Swansons were raising cattle, having given up years before on trying to raise sheep and remain solvent.

It took some cows to cook my goose!

On one of my first visits to the farm Ardie decided I would benefit from an elementary lesson in working with cows. Because of the terrain on the farm, it took a lot of land for all the cows to graze. That usually meant a long walk at milking time, through brushland and woods, over and around streams, to round up the cows and head them back to the barn.

Bringing in the cows sounded easy to me, and it seemed like a way to make some positive points with both Ardie and her father, Albert. One evening I set out on my mission. I had to follow a roundabout route since the most direct way was blocked by a wide, deep stream. After following the stream for a considerable distance, I found a place where it narrowed enough to jump across.

I finally tracked down the cows, which were lazily grazing in a meadow. It didn't take long to get them moving and ambling toward home. As we entered the wooded area, some of the thirty cows moved out of my sight, but I could hear their hooves crunching through twigs and leaves.

To my surprise, when the cows in front of me reached the stream, they opted for the shortcut, swimming across easily. The creek was about fifteen feet wide, but the cows had no problem. Not excited about retracing my earlier detour, I wondered if there wasn't a way I could follow the animals. I noticed a limb of a nearby tree extending conveniently over the water. Surely, I thought, I can grab it and swing to the other side without getting wet!

I took hold of the limb and swung forward, doing my best Tarzan impersonation. Midway across the stream, the limb snapped, depositing me unceremoniously into the water. Although the water was several feet over my head, I quickly returned to the surface and swam to the opposite bank.

Pulling myself out of the stream, every bit of me— including my wallet and boots—was thoroughly soaked. Despite the setback, however, I felt pleased. I had succeeded in gathering the cows together and kept up with them as they headed back to the barn. I anticipated a good appraisal from Ardie and her father.

My sense of self-satisfaction was dampened, however, as I spotted Ardie standing atop a nearby hill. Instead of words of encouragement, she shouted, "Ken, you don't have all the cows!"

My first impulse was to yell back, "Forget the cows!" but I knew that wasn't the right answer. Dutifully I turned back, taking the long—but dry—way, to find and herd the remaining bovine fugitives into the barn.

Later, Ardie's father offered this assessment: "Ken, I don't believe you'll ever make a good farmer, but then, I'd probably never make a good phone man."

Fortunately, Ardie was able to overlook the fact that I once was led astray by a cow, and she married me two years later.

While raising my sheep, it was interesting to observe that sheep don't have to learn how to follow the leader. They do it instinctively, practically from birth. Any shepherd (traditional or three-piece suit variety) enjoys watching new lambs on their first days of "freedom" from the barn. Since our lambs were always born while it was still cold, we kept them confined in the barn with their mothers until warmer days arrived. That meant each lamb's "world" for the first weeks of its life consisted of a pen with dimensions of about five feet by five feet. Even for a lamb that is not much space, especially when it must be shared with "Mom."

With the coming of warm weather, we would send the ewes and their lambs into the pastures. The immediate surprise and delight of the little ones was evident. They would romp into the open spaces, expending their pent-up energy. After a quick glance to make sure their mothers were not far away, the lambs would gather in a group to play.

The pasture became a playground paradise for them. Happily they would run from one side to another, rolling and tumbling in the fresh grass, scampering as fast as their little legs permitted. After a time they would pause on one side of the pasture. Suddenly one lamb would break for the opposite side and just as quickly, the other lambs would be in pursuit.

As they explored the pasture, they often would discover a tiny hill. One lamb would decide to become "king of the hill," until his friends would join him. It was comical to see fifteen lambs each squirming for a space on the little hill, demonstrating that it is not always lonely at the top! After standing still for a few moments, the lambs would look at each other as if to say, "What do we do now?" Almost instantly, a lamb would charge off the hill, heading for another section of the pasture, and the others again would eagerly follow. They didn't know where they were going, but they were not going to be left behind.

Force of habit can be a strong motivator

As I think about it, I am amazed how much we are like those little lambs in our daily activities. Many of our revered, established traditions today continue long after their original reasons have ceased to exist. For instance, many evangelical churches have regular Sunday night services in addition to morning worship. I wholeheartedly support that practice, but do you know how Sunday evening services got started? Believe it or not, it wasn't because someone decided one Lord's Day service was not enough.

Actually, the credit must go to the dynamic duo of evangelism—and gas lights! In the early nineteenth century, gas lights were too expensive for most private homes. As a result people were fascinated by the new innovation and flocked to public buildings where the artificial illumination could transform night into day. To capitalize on the curiosity, ministers in many churches had gas lights installed in their sanctuaries and began conducting Sunday evening services, primarily to attract the unchurched members of their community and give them an opportunity to hear the gospel message.[1]

More than 150 years later, thousands upon thousands throng to their churches on Sunday nights, most of them totally unaware of the original purpose for those meetings.

We could cite numerous other examples of tried-and-true traditions which have lost sight of their reason for existence, but having a better understanding of our "follow the leader" tendencies, I believe we can learn two important concepts. First of all, we become more aware of the "I don't want to try anything new" attitude. Many traditions certainly deserve to be maintained, but maybe we need to question those established practices to determine whether they are still worth keeping. A few probing questions could help: "Why are we doing it this way?" "Is there a better, more effective way?" "Does this have a real purpose, or are we just clinging to a comfortable old habit?"

Some years ago, I learned a business principle called, "Going outside the nine dots." As you see in the diagram, there are nine dots in the shape of a square, lined up in rows of three. The challenge is to connect the nine dots by using only four lines—and not lifting your pen or pencil once you have started drawing the lines.

• • •

• • •

• • •

Inc. magazine, March 1981, p. 143.

At first you puzzle over the problem, and may even conclude it cannot be done. If you restrict your thinking to within those nine dots, that is a correct analysis. No matter how you try, one or more dots will remain unconnected. However, if you extend your lines outside the nine dots, the puzzle can indeed be solved.

Have you ever had a situation like that at work? A problem occurs, and no solution seems to work. You agonize over your dilemma to no avail. Then an associate suggests an idea that, at first, seems totally outside the realm of possibility. Very soon, however, you realize that although it is beyond the framework you had been working in, the proposed solution is perfectly acceptable. It is simply a fresh approach, a completely different, but simple angle to the dilemma that had baffled you.

My second lesson from my sheepish friends is that we need to be sure we are following the right leader. Jesus Christ summed it up best when He said, "If anyone wishes to come after Me, let him deny himself, and take up his cross daily, and follow Me" (Luke 9:23).

That doesn't leave much room for compromise. And it's interesting to me that Christ did not offer any exceptions such as "except in business" or "except with the family" or "except when you get an offer you can't refuse." Instead, He repeatedly points out that from His perspective we are sheep, He is "the good shepherd" (John 10:11). We have a variety of shepherds from which to choose, but there is only one "good shepherd," Jesus says. We'll look at some of the "alternative shepherds" in the next chapters.

THOUGHTS TO CONSIDER AND DISCUSS:

1. When was the last time you played "follow the leader"? In what ways does society encourage us to continue following that pattern, even as adults?

2. We are all creatures of habit to some degree. Think of an example in your life when you have done something without asking, "Why?" At work, at home, or even in church. Are you threatened by new ideas or breaking with old traditions and routines?

3. What is a problem you are facing presently which might best be resolved by going "outside the nine dots"? Looking at Isaiah 55:8, how might your relationship with God help in finding a solution?

FOOTNOTES

[1] *The Seven Last Words of the Church* by Ralph Neighbor © 1973, Zondervan Publishing House, Grand Rapids, Michigan.

Solution to nine-dot problem (from page 44)

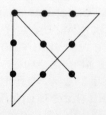

CHAPTER FOUR

YOU HAVE TO SET A GOOD EXAMPLE

"My people have become lost sheep; their shepherds have led them astray."
—Jeremiah 50:6—

When was the last time you heard of an adult getting lost because he was following a child? I can't remember ever hearing of such a thing. An experienced shepherd knows the same is true of his flock. A mature sheep will not go off track by following a lamb; however, an adventuresome or disobedient ram or ewe can lead other members of the flock astray. One sheep following his nose toward the beckoning horizon literally can lead his companions down a path of destruction. That kind of leader a shepherd cannot afford to have!

What is a shepherd's recourse when he discovers a recalcitrant rascal in his midst? Sheep experts agree there is but one sure cure: Get rid of the troublesome individual! It may seem harsh, but the welfare of the flock is worth far more than the aggravations of battling continually with a chronic bad example.

Whenever I think of sheep like this—and we had a few during our fourteen years of shepherding—I'm reminded of one of my favorite parables in the Bible. Jesus' story in Matthew 18 about the "ninety and nine" actually focuses on one such independent sheep, the one who strayed and became lost.

What do you think? If any man has a hundred sheep, and one of them has gone astray, does he not leave the ninety-nine on the mountains and go and search for the one that is straying? And if it turns out that he finds it, truly I say to you, he rejoices over it more than over the ninety-nine which have not gone astray (verses 12-13).

In this story, we see not only a shepherd's great love and devotion to each member of his flock, but also Christ's unlimited and unconditional love for His children. This parable is a great source of assurance and security for me, and reaffirms how important each one of us is to God.

Jesus' account, however, offers us more than an account about a wayward sheep. I believe it is significant that He spoke about an adult animal, not a lamb, and reminds us of the responsibility and influence we have upon the "lambs" around us.

Lambs rarely venture very far from their mothers. In the last chapter I told you how the young lambs, even though they were enjoying their new freedom in the open pasture, always kept their moms in sight. That served two purposes: They maintained the sense of security they had enjoyed in the barn, and they also knew when their internal dinner bells sounded, that they were close to the "cafeteria."

An adult sheep is far more independent and generally can find his own food. It is when he wanders off, either in search of a more varied diet or to satisfy his curiosity, that he can stir up trouble—for himself and others. If he has some status in the flock and is accepted by his peers as a leader, you may soon have more than one lost sheep to track down!

Years ago, Thomas Spurgeon put the dilemma to verse:

'Twas a Sheep, Not a Lamb

It was a sheep—not a lamb, that strayed away,
In the parable Jesus told:
A grown-up sheep that had gone astray
From the ninety and nine in the fold.

Out in the meadows, out in the cold,
'Twas a sheep the good Shepherd sought.
Back to the flock and into the fold,
'Twas a sheep the good Shepherd brought.

And why for the sheep, should we earnestly long,
And so earnestly hope and pray?
Because there is danger, if they go wrong,
They will lead the young lambs away.

For the lambs follow the sheep, you know,
Wherever the sheep may stray;
If the sheep go wrong, it will not be long
Till the lambs are as wrong as they.

So with the sheep we earnestly plead,
For the sake of the lambs today.
If the lambs are lost, what a terrible cost,
Some sheep may have to pay!

Relating this to the human level, we don't have to

think very long to list several examples of leadership which resulted in tragedy. Adolf Hitler at one time was well-regarded; many German citizens unquestioningly followed his direction, even when his murderous objectives became evident. Because of that one "sheep," millions of men, women, and children literally were led to the slaughter.

A more recent case is that of Rev. Jim Jones who, at first, appeared to be a sincere man, dedicated to serving God. Years later, Jones assumed the role of his own god and led a holocaust, guiding 913 people to their deaths in Jonestown, Guyana in 1978. A list of other monstrous personalities could fill the remainder of this book. Only time will reveal the impact of more recent leadership tragedies.

The role of "shepherd" carries great responsibility

These grim events of history vividly illustrate the consequences of following the wrong sheep. Equally important, these tragedies also demonstrate the great responsibility we bear whenever we have the opportunity to serve as shepherds or leaders for others.

In the book of I Peter (5:2-3), we are told to, "...shepherd the flock of God among you, not under compulsion, but voluntarily...proving to be examples to the flock." During my shepherding days I discovered a secret to effective leadership: To guide the sheep, you need a "sheep magnet." This was not an actual magnet, but rather a bucket of feed or water. Unlike human beings, sheep are not impressed by the externals of personal appearance, but a bucket which promises a treat—even a dented or rusty bucket—generally gains a sheep's total attention.

After a time it is not the bucket's contents, but the promise of the contents, that lures the sheep. Once they have learned it may contain grain or water, even an empty bucket will bring them running. Anytime I wanted to get my flock's attention, I would grab a bucket and rattle it a couple times. It never failed to draw them to me.

Once the sheep have learned to associate their shepherd with the beckoning bucket, they start to follow the shepherd even when he doesn't have the bucket. A sense of trust and dependence has been established, and the sheep develop a close association with their leader.

Of course, sheep—like people—occasionally need proper behavior reinforced if it is to continue. Therefore, from time to time I would let them have the bucket instead of just dangling it in front of them. A sheep, in its enthusiasm to consume the grain, would stick its head deep into the bucket. Sometimes the handle would get caught around the sheep's neck and over its ears, sending the animal into a fit of perplexity.

Sheep, not being an analytical species, do not have a simple solution to the question, "What do you do when you have accidentally gotten the bucket handle caught around your neck?" The general response is to do what comes most natural—run around the pasture in a blind panic in the truest sense. If you think a sheep in that condition is easy to catch, just try it some day!

Again applying our principles to people, the idea of "bucket leadership" is relevant. To be a leader you need followers, and to have followers, you must offer something that is attractive and appealing. This is true of political parties, which offer specific platforms and ideologies for their loyal supporters. This characteristic also explains in large measure the fascination some people have with religious cults which promise to meet such human needs as love, peace, acceptance, purpose, and a sense of belonging.

In the workplace, the quality of leadership frequently determines the success or failure of a project, or even an entire company. While I was with the telephone company, one man particularly impressed me as a strong and able leader. Actually, he was my boss's boss, but I had the chance to observe him in action a number of times. Interestingly, what made him most effective as a leader was not his ability to enforce his orders, but his obviously sincere concern for people. People usually are interested in someone who is interested in them. This man set high expectations for his workers and was very demanding, but he also was fair and supportive of his employees. His result? A high level of loyalty and commitment from all of them.

As I advanced to new management positions, this man's compassion and sensitivity served as an example for me. One day stands out in particular for me. I had just been transferred from Cloquet, Minnesota to Duluth. The cities were just twenty miles apart, but we had a heavy snow and there was no way for me to return home. Everything was at a standstill in the city for two days—except for telephone problems, which not only continued but intensified.

I had to get a room at a hotel, but I had not been prepared for an overnight stay. Without being asked, this executive—who was not even my immediate superior—brought me a clean shirt, toothbrush, and razor. It was a simple act, but his thoughtfulness left an impression.

I haven't always succeeded, but I've tried in similar ways to acknowledge extra effort by people who have worked for me. One winter the telephone lines near Cloquet required some complicated circuitry work. The project had to be done at night to avoid disrupting telephone service. I did not have to do any of the work personally, but I was responsible for supervising the work.

Leadership is more than a warm feeling

We were living in the town and it was a bitterly cold night, the kind that makes you especially thankful for a warm, well-insulated house. As I sat in the living room and looked through the window, I could see the snow blowing outside and hear the wind buffeting our house. On TV, the weatherman reported the temperature was ten degrees below zero and advised, "It's a good night to stay inside and off the roads."

As he said that, an image flashed through my mind of the meager canvas enclosure that was the only protection for one of my three-men crews working forty miles to the north. The mere thought of venturing into the cold caused me to shiver, but I felt I should do something for the men to show my appreciation for their work under such adverse conditions. At the phone company our slogan was, "The Spirit of Service," and on that night my work crew was living out that motto.

It was close to midnight, but I put on my coat and—after assuring Ardie I was not suffering from frostbite of the brain—got into my car and drove to a restaurant in Cloquet to buy a bag of hamburgers for the men. It was the pre-McDonald's era, and I had the waitress pack the sandwiches tightly to keep them warm. Then I got back into my car and drove toward the work site.

Technically, the men were not my crew. They had been temporarily assigned to my area, but since I was in charge of overseeing the special project, I felt responsible for the men's welfare. When I arrived, the men were puzzled. They had heard my car crunching across the snow-crusted roadway. The nearest town was twenty miles away, and understandably, there was not a lot of competing noise that evening. Since it was unlikely that anyone would take a leisurely drive at that hour or under those conditions, they could not imagine who was coming when they heard my car creak to a stop at the side of the road.

Walking the short distance in the drifted snow, I announced, "Men, I've got some goodies for you!" They had not been expecting a delivery man from Hamburger Haven, but the hamburgers were welcomed and eagerly consumed.

As it turned out, that scheduled three-week project was completed one week early. I'm sure the frigid weather hastened the work pace considerably, but I'd like to think that their morale, boosted by warm burgers on a cold night, helped motivate them as well. To this day, Jim Broman, who headed the crew, is one of my best friends.

The cold weather in Minnesota made a habit of presenting opportunities to demonstrate special kindnesses to telephone company employees. There was another severe snowstorm in Duluth, blocking most of the roads in and out of town. Phone and power lines were down all over the city.

Desperately laboring to restore phone communications as quickly as possible, my crews worked through the evening and into the night. It was the normal procedure to get them something to eat, but I felt this particular crisis called for something special. The men were doing first-class work under extremely difficult circumstances. I wanted them to know their diligence was not going unnoticed.

I called the best nearby restaurant and ordered twenty filet mignon dinners to go, with everything. It was an unusual order, especially "to go," but the restaurant promptly complied. When I delivered the steaks, the only thing that warded off the men's shock at seeing the dinners was the hunger they had worked up by their frantic efforts to restore phone service. They were so excited after devouring that dinner, I believe they would have worked another two days straight if I had asked them.

Sheep reproduce sheep; shepherds don't

A basic truth is that sheep reproduce sheep, not the shepherd. During the years I tended to the sheep, I never produced one. Yet the shepherd has a vital influence upon the flock. We often single out the villains of history as examples of bad leaders, but we should not underestimate the disastrous impact of "normal people" who fail to recognize the seriousness of their role as shepherds to people around them.

This can happen in the workplace, where an

insensitive, domineering boss can destroy company morale and eventually drive away quality, talented people. It can occur in a church where a minister falls into immoral behavior and disgrace, disillusioning members of his congregation. Poor leadership has a particularly profound influence in the home, where children imitate the actions of the parents they love.

I have to admit I often forget that I am constantly serving as an example to my children. One Saturday when Janelle was six-years-old, we went for a leisurely drive. I was absorbed in the lovely scenery when she tapped me on the shoulder. "Dad, aren't you going a little too fast?" I was indeed. Going a few miles above the speed limit hardly classified me as a felon, but her reminder helped me to see the importance of serving as a model in even the seemingly little details of life.

Another time our youngest daughter, Jolene, was sitting with us at the kitchen table. We were engaged in a family project, memorizing Bible verses. I was reviewing a passage with Jim when Jolene, who had just turned four, spoke up. "I want to try one," she announced. At first I didn't respond, thinking she was too young to memorize. But when she repeated her desire, I said, "Okay, Jolene. Let's hear your verse." She promptly recited the reference, II Corinthians 5:17, and then repeated the verse perfectly! I was amazed. What was most interesting was we had not realized she was even paying attention, yet she had followed our example precisely.

It has been said that whatever a parent does in moderation, a child will do in excess. This is a sobering thought when we consider some of the things we do routinely, hoping consciously or subconsciously that our offspring will never duplicate them.

Looking at the positive side of a shepherd's influence, there are many men and women I have admired over the years. They have taught me a lot, but I have realized also that they are imperfect human beings, just as I am. As the book of Romans states, "There is none righteous, not even one" (3:10).

We select our shepherds—the leaders we follow—by how they look, their charisma, cleverness of speech, intelligence, or skills and talents in certain areas. Often we pattern our own leadership styles after them. But the danger is that in patterning ourselves after imperfection, the best we can achieve is that level of imperfection.

I have realized over and over that, for human "sheep," there is ultimately only one Shepherd we can follow who is totally dependable, only one who serves as a perfect model. Jesus Christ said, "I am the good shepherd; and I know My own, and My own know Me, even as the Father knows Me and I know the Father; and I lay down My life for the sheep" (John 10:14-15).

At our Lake Elmo home, whenever we had visitors we would show off our sheep. Almost every time the guest would call the sheep; if he didn't, I would encourage him to do so. Regardless of what he said or how he called, the visitor could not get the sheep's attention. After a few minutes, I would make a quick noise, not very loud. Instantly, the sheep would raise their heads and look our way. As Jesus said of the shepherd, "the sheep hear his voice, and he calls his own sheep by name, and leads them out...and the sheep follow him because they know his voice" (John 10:3-4).

Sheep are smart enough to know who their shepherd

57

is and respond only to him. We need that same wisdom. In today's world we have countless would-be shepherds for our human flock, but Jesus is the only one we can trust completely—with our very lives and our eternal souls. He said, "If any one wishes to come after Me, let him deny himself, and take up his cross, and follow Me" (Matthew 16:24).

THOUGHTS TO CONSIDER AND DISCUSS:

1. How do we determine who is a leader? List what you would consider to be good leadership qualities.

2. One of the examples Jesus Christ gave us was that of a "servant leader." What are some ways a leader can serve those who work for him? (II Corinthians 4:5)

3. Who are some of the leaders you presently follow? Why? What biblical characteristics of leadership do they have? What human characteristics? (See I Corinthians 4:15-16.)

CHAPTER FIVE

IF YOU FEEL LIKE GIVING UP, DON'T

"And seeing the multitudes, He felt compassion for them, because they were distressed and downcast like sheep without a shepherd."
—Matthew 9:36—

Our veterinarian in Lake Elmo had a saying: "A sick sheep is a dead sheep." Generally he was right. Whenever a ewe or lamb seemed ill, we would try to treat it or have the vet come by and take a look, but in most cases our flock would be diminished by one within a few days.

There are two major reasons for that. First, once a sheep becomes ill, its resistance becomes very low and it recovers very slowly. If you want hardy, resilient animals, sheep are not the ones to have.

The second reason is a simple economic consideration. Once a lamb becomes diseased, it could cost several hundred dollars to nurse it back to health. Since a fair market price for a ewe ranges from thirty-five to fifty dollars, it makes little business sense to invest a lot of money in a sick sheep. With an already low profit margin in the sheep industry, sentimentality has no place—especially when you have dozens of other sheep to care for and maintain.

However, sheep will surprise you occasionally. One evening after returning home from work, I discovered an ailing ewe in the barn. She seemed more than half dead. Lying on her side, her breathing was labored and irregular; her eyes were watering; there was foam around her mouth, and she had a bloated appearance. Her days of producing wool sweaters had ended, I concluded.

I called the veterinarian, and he came to examine the animal. He shook his head as he looked her over. Her chances of living through the night, he said, were virtually nonexistent. Almost an as afterthought, he gave the ewe a shot of medication, reasoning that it might help and certainly would not do any harm. He was honest as he left. "I'm afraid I just cost you some money for nothing."

The next morning I decided to dispose of the poor sheep before I began the daily chores. From her condition the previous evening, I had no doubt she was lying dead in the barn. I was so certain I took a shovel from the shed as I left the house and walked to the field to select a spot to bury the ewe. It took an hour of hard, steady work to dig the grave. When the hole was completed, I went to the barn to collect the carcass.

Nearing the barn, I could hear the persistent bleating of a sheep eager to get out to the pasture. I was shocked to find the "dead" ewe very much alive. That morning she looked as healthy as any of the other members of my flock! In a moment or two I recovered from my surprise and remembered I was still holding the shovel

I had used to dig the intended grave. I felt a bit sheepish myself as I quickly hid the tool behind my back, not wanting the ewe to know I had expected anything less than a complete recovery.

Proving her return to health was no fluke, that ewe lived a full lifespan. (We usually kept our ewes about six years before we sold them.) She also bore several lambs for us over the next years, teaching me the value of never giving up on sheep—or people.

A shepherd must watch for changes in his flock

One of a shepherd's most important responsibilities is the well-being of his sheep. He must be a practiced observer of his flock so if something goes wrong, he can take immediate action. As the Bible says in Proverbs 27:23, "Know well the condition of your flocks, and pay attention to your herds."

A good shepherd is quick to detect any significant changes among his flock—a limping ewe, a sheep not eating properly, perhaps one that seems unusually restless. Often the problem is minor, caused by a thorn in a foot, wire wrapped around a leg, or ligaments strained by stepping into a hole. But sheep are totally helpless and fully dependent upon the shepherd's diligent care.

A great asset for a shepherd in spotting troubles is becoming an expert at what a problem-free sheep looks like. A normal, healthy sheep has a straight back; its ribs do not protrude; its wool coat is even, dense and full, without any gaps. It is active and lively but not overly agitated; its eyes and nose are clear; it moves easily with the group, and eats eagerly. The absence of any one of these characteristics may signal a problem, and the shepherd must respond immediately.

In the opening chapter I told you about the ewe with the difficult delivery. That illustrated my disadvantage in being a part-time shepherd. Most of our lambs had been born normally, with many deliveries occurring while I was at work. Had I been more experienced in observing ewes as their time was nearing, I might have realized in advance that the ewe was going to need help.

Interestingly, acquiring skill at recognizing the real thing is the same philosophy used by the U.S. government in training people to spot counterfeit currency. A friend of mine, a former Army Finance Department officer, told me about the intensive drills agents go through in learning to distinguish bogus bills from the authentic. I was surprised to discover, however, that probably 90 percent of their time is spent in examining real money. They study the genuine article in infinite detail, reviewing intricate markings and characteristics over and over again. The key is concentrating upon the real thing. Only during the final hours of the grueling seminars do they finally get to inspect counterfeit money. By that time they are so familiar with bonafide currency that fakes can be spotted very quickly.

I found this principle also had application in business. As a phone company supervisor, I saw an importance in keeping watch over my employees, not because I distrusted them, but because I was concerned for their personal and vocational welfare.

Each of my people, in my view, was part of a team and a hurting team member is a serious concern. From a business standpoint, many times an employee's problems detract from his performance and directly or indirectly hinder the team's overall effort. Even more importantly, I believe employers have an obligation to extend a helping hand whenever possible to those working for them.

As with sheep, there are a multitude of problems that can affect employees. It might be personal illness, marital conflict and other family crises, or financial pressures. Increasing alcoholism and drug abuse are being confronted in the workplace. The sooner the problems can be spotted and help provided, the greater the chance of recovery and return to productivity. But like the shepherd watching his sheep and the government agent scrutinizing genuine currency, the employer needs to know his workers well enough under normal conditions so that when difficulties appear, they become evident and can be dealt with properly.

I try to observe that principle in our home as well. I've discovered that to be an effective, supportive husband, I need to spend an ample amount of time with my wife. After years of knowing how Ardie acts when things are going well, I can usually sense when something is wrong and try to determine if there is anything I need to do to help her.

Occasionally we hear of people who say they were caught totally by surprise when a spouse asked for a divorce. Obviously, when people get married they don't plan to get divorced. Something happens to shatter the hopes and expectations they had on the wedding day. For the husband whose wife demands a divorce "all of a sudden," he has made a very serious error: He failed to heed the advice of the proverb to "know well the condition of your flock."

The same concept applies to a father's relationship with his children. In the business world, we face continual pressures. Money, success, and prestige all beckon to us. There is nothing intrinsically wrong with any of those, unless we pursue them at the expense of our more important and immediate responsibilities— our families and our relationship with the Lord.

I have known men who could not believe it when they learned a son or daughter had been arrested for a crime, or had become addicted to drugs or alcohol. But when we consider how little time the average father spends with his children—mere minutes a week according to some experts—surprise is understandable. When a father doesn't spend enough time with his children, he can easily fail to notice when something is wrong. While the father is spending most of his waking hours climbing the ladder of success with the conviction, "I'm really doing all this for my family," his family may be suffering from neglect and virtual abandonment. That is not the way of a good shepherd!

> There is a need
> to count—
> and to be counted on

In many businesses, taking inventory is a regularly scheduled activity. The same is true for the shepherd. Some people count sheep at night to sleep. I counted sheep during the day while fully awake, intent on making sure all of my sheep were accounted for and in good condition.

You could say that sheep are the equivalent of Murphy's Law in long woolen outerwear. Whatever can go wrong, will. Knowing the many misfortunes that can befall his sheep is a continual concern for the shepherd. Sheep can wander off into another pasture and get lost. Their heads may get stuck in a fence—one consequence of the greener grass syndrome. They can become sick or injured by stumbling or being attacked by another animal. Or, they can be rendered totally helpless in a potentially life-threatening condition which is called being "cast."

Occasionally, one of our sheep would go for a stroll in an unfamiliar area, oblivious to potential hazards it might encounter. Especially dangerous, curiously enough, were depressions in the ground from as little as one inch deep to as much as one foot deep. When a sheep stepped into such a natural hazard, it could stumble, lose its balance, flip over, and find itself lying upside down—all four feet pointed toward the sky.

When it gets in that position, usually a sheep is unable to turn itself over. This is the case with a number of breeds, including the Southdowns we had, because of their bone structure and the cushiony nature of a thick coat of wool. When the sheep fall onto their backs, the wool is matted flat against the ground. With their short legs of no use, they become utterly helpless no matter how much they struggle and wiggle.

That condition is being "cast"; the sheep's only hope is the prompt arrival and assistance of its shepherd. Without help, the sheep can die within a few hours— particularly in hot weather. In that unnatural position, gases accumulate within the sheep which eventually cause it to suffocate.

Sometimes I would discover a sheep's dilemma very quickly and hurry to its aid. All that was needed to end the crisis was a slight nudge, enabling the sheep to turn onto its side. In moments it would be back on its feet, shake its head, and then walk away as if nothing had happened. Unfortunately, there were a few times when too many hours had elapsed, and I would discover a sheep still on its back, dead. All because of the lack of a helpful push!

In the Bible verse at the beginning of this chapter, Jesus Christ saw the people as "...downcast like sheep without a shepherd." In a literal sense, He saw them as lying belly up and helpless.

Have you ever felt like that? You tried everything you could imagine, yet nothing seemed to work? Perhaps you had reached an impasse in a difficult business situation. Or perhaps a family problem seemed insurmountable. Frustrated, you are reluctant to make any decision for fear it might be wrong. At such times, rather than making a bad choice, it appears a wiser course to do nothing at all.

I have found that even in some extremely perplexing circumstances, all I needed was a little nudge, much like the sheep lying on its back. Perhaps a business associate can offer some helpful insight, analyzing a situation from a slightly different perspective—going outside the nine dots—and pointing to a solution. At other times, all we need is a word of encouragement, the gentle sort of nudge that rechannels our thoughts from the negative track and back on to the positive.

'Cast sheep' can be found right in our own homes

Now that we have moved south, leaving our flock behind, I no longer scour pastures in search of cast sheep. However, recalling the help I received when I became "cast," I know I still need to watch for downcast people. They might even live in my own home.

When we moved to Chattanooga, the transition was relatively simple for me. I had the excitement of a new job, and I was working with a number of people I already knew well. The change was harder for my family, particularly for Janelle who, by that time, was a teenager and midway through high school. It had been difficult for her to leave old friends, favorite activities, and familiar places. Ardie and I made a point of talking with her often, encouraging her to look upon our move as a positive experience. Once she made new friends her attitude changed, but I know she needed the assurance of our love and concern for her.

I don't succeed as much as I would like, but I work at giving my family the proper place in my life. The Bible teaches that our priorities should be God first, wife and family second, and only then, vocation. Yet, in our society where so much of our identity and sense of self-worth is bound up in our work, it is a temptation to move our jobs up to the No. 2 priority, or even No. 1. (I try to keep in mind the Scripture passage that points out if a man does not care for his family, he is "worse than an infidel"—I Timothy 5:8). Therefore, before I try playing good Samaritan and go looking for fallen sheep outside of our home, I need to make sure there are no "cast" members of the Johnson flock.

At work I feel I have a similar responsibility. There is a need to recognize people as individuals with needs, not as instruments for achieving goals and objectives. In American business circles, we often say our most valuable resource is people, but the tendency is to pay more attention to our machines and tools than we do to our employees! The problem is, machines don't become cast but people do.

As a manager in business I saw how important this was. Employees who are healthy physically, mentally, and emotionally are far more productive, and they respond with their best efforts when they know their leader has a genuine interest in their welfare. Management by manipulation may work in the short term, but its long-term impact can be devastating.

It's been interesting to me that at those times when I start to forget my duties as a shepherd at home and at work, my children have a way of reminding me. Back in Lake Elmo, it often amazed me how much better my children knew our sheep than I did. Jim or Janelle would point to a ewe and report, "Hey, Dad, I think that one is going to have a lamb next." I would reply, "Oh, yeah?" conceding that most of the time I couldn't tell. The kids usually were very accurate. "Johnson," I would think to myself, "you're not as good an observer as you think you are."

How about the "flocks" for which you are responsible? Have you been watching as diligently as you should? I learned that you never know when you'll come across a cast sheep. Prompt attention can make a lot of difference. As they say, prevention is always preferable to the cure.

THOUGHTS TO CONSIDER AND DISCUSS:

1. When the going gets tough, it's easy to give up. Can you think of an instance when you gave up in the face of a tough situation and later felt you should have tried harder? What about a time when you did persevere and were glad you did?

2. How would you go about recognizing a "sick lamb" in your own sphere of influence—at home, on the job, or in your church family? Read I Peter 5:2-3.

3. In your family or business, can you think of any "counterfeits" you are accepting at the expense of the authentic? Consider the instructions in Philippians 4:8.

— CHAPTER SIX —

DON'T LET THEM PULL THE WOOL OVER YOUR EYES

"Then I will give you shepherds after My own heart, who will feed you on knowledge and understanding."
—Jeremiah 3:15—

Have you ever wondered where the old saying, "Don't let them pull the wool over your eyes," came from? Like the "grass is greener" and some of our other familiar cliches, I believe it started with an observant, practical-minded shepherd.

All sheep grow wool, but not all sheep grow wool equally. Most of the time on our farm we raised a breed of sheep called Suffolk. The short-haired, black muzzles of the Suffolks made for a striking contrast to their cream-colored coats of wool, particularly just before shearing time.

However, another type of sheep we had for awhile, called Southdown, grew wool everywhere, even over its face. This distinctive breed literally would have the wool pulled over its eyes by the natural process of growth. To remedy this problem, we would trim the wool from their faces regularly. Otherwise, the plentiful wool would droop over their foreheads and around their eyes. I suppose it would be like trying to walk with a thick wool sweater over your head. Unless we responded promptly with the clippers, our sheep would have difficulty seeing where they were going or finding food.

The warning about having wool pulled over one's eyes may have been a readily understood expression among shepherds to remind one another to guard against dishonest transactions with other people. By observing their sheep, they had learned well the hazards of obscured vision.

Generally, the problem of wool over the eyes for humans is far more subtle. It can be a result of intended deception or simply our own lack of awareness. In my thirty plus years of driving automobiles, few things have been more frustrating than trying to maneuver through a thick fog. You don't know what lies ahead, and you aren't sure what may be approaching from behind. We can experience the same effect when we are weighing an important decision. The way may seem clouded as we search for the right path, and we can empathize with the poor Southdown sheep whose negligent shepherd has forgotten to cut away the bothersome wool.

One reason we may have trouble dealing with circumstances present and future is due to our difficulty in viewing them objectively and honestly. This type of blindness can be as disabling as that of the woolly-eyed Southdown. We may truly be helpless to remove this "wool." What can we do?

For me, the answer is found in the form of personal

accountability to another individual or a small group of men. A person whom I trust and who knows me well—much like the relationship between sheep and their shepherd—can be very helpful in pointing out problems and blind spots, some of which can be surprisingly obvious to someone else.

> There is a subtle
> danger in not
> being accountable

This concept was first presented to me after I became involved in Christian Business Men's Committee in 1970. One of the immediate benefits for me was being able to meet with other Christian businessmen and discuss common concerns and interests. As I developed close friendships with some of the men, we began to build accountability into our relationship. We would openly discuss problems and needs, offering encouragement, but we also felt the freedom to challenge one another if we felt someone had gotten off track in a particular area.

Like the times when I would trim the obstructing wool from around the eyes of my sheep, we would help one another to put biblical principles into action, pointing out any instances in which we might not be seeing clearly. At times we would admonish one another boldly, using God's Word as our source of authority, whether the problem concerned our spiritual growth, business practices, or family relationships.

I'm convinced that one reason many people are struggling in their lives today is that they have no one to remove the wool from their eyes. They are not accountable to anyone, so there is no one to point out their shortcomings or other critical areas that need attention.

It was in the context of accountability that CBMC indirectly prompted my decision to leave the telephone company in 1971. Once a week a group of us businessmen would meet for prayer and Bible study. One of the men I had met there was Chuck McKenzie, the president and owner of a small service company. He desired to become more involved in Christian work as a layman, but his business responsibilities greatly restricted his free time.

While we were discussing this, I flippantly suggested, "Why don't you get more involved, and I'll run the business for you?" I said that in jest. I had enjoyed my years at the phone company, but I knew very little about Chuck's business which involved the remanufacture of acetylene-oxygen welding equipment and medical regulators used in hospitals. Chuck didn't realize I was joking, however, and surprised me by accepting my offer.

Six weeks later, after prayer and much deliberation, I found myself making a major job transition. Suddenly, instead of supervising a crew of approximately one hundred people maintaining telephone service for St. Paul and adjacent suburbs, I was learning how to run a company of just twenty employees. It was a traumatic change for awhile. At first I didn't even have a desk of my own, but the move proved to be a good one. The challenge of running a different business was stimulating, and both Chuck and I were able to devote more time to Christian activities.

Sometimes parasites require a closer examination

Wool covering the eyes was not the only annoyance for my sheep. Ticks, small parasites that would bore through the wool and into the sheep's bodies, were another nagging problem. The ticks could reproduce quickly and, before long, the entire flock would be infested.

Hosting a heavy population of ticks can be debilitating for a sheep. It becomes run down physically, and the quality of its wool diminishes as a result. Because of their thick wool, our sheep often had to be in a state of obviously declining health before we would discover the ticks and step in to combat them.

Today, the ticks can be eliminated fairly easily by spraying the sheep with newly developed insecticides. But when we were raising our sheep, it was not so simple. We had to dip our sheep in a special solution, putting them into a tank we converted from a 55-gallon drum. The greatest difficulty was getting the sheep to cooperate. They particularly disliked having their heads dunked into the liquid, but it was necessary to kill the ticks and put our animals on recovery road.

As a shepherd, I knew the experience was not pleasant for the sheep. It may even have been frightening to be suddenly submerged into a chemical solution. Having no way to explain our intentions, though, we just forced the animals to comply.

With the sheep, the troubling ticks were literally closer than skin, since they would burrow beneath the skin's surface. In spite of that, the sheep appeared unaware of their plight. It took an outsider—their shepherd—to notice something was wrong, prescribe, and carry out procedures to rectify the problem. Even if our sheep had understood the situation, they would not have known what to do about it.

In business we sometimes undertake programs that are similar to dipping the sheep. We may call in consultants (formerly called "efficiency experts") to observe and see if there are any "ticks" in our system. Sometimes, even though we know their recommendations are for our ultimate good, we strongly resist any corrective measures due to immediate uncertainties.

Many businessmen have a tendency to "wing it," taking the attitude that, "It's my company, and I'm going to run it my way!" Frequently, that type of attitude can prove self-destructive. These entrepreneurs may have excellent products or services to offer, but due to a lack of good advice, their businesses can falter and eventually fail.

That is one reason it is so important for any business or organization to have a board of advisors, concerned but not intimately tied to it. Both Proverbs 11:14 and 15:22 tell us about the wisdom to be gained from many counselors. They are the people who can spot the "ticks" afflicting us even when we are oblivious to them. Too often we make a mistake in thinking we have to be accountable to no one. Christians are commanded ultimately to be accountable to God, and if we expect our plans to succeed, our best hope is through accountability to others who have a sincere concern for us.

This concept of accountability is applicable in the home as well. Sometimes a family problem may persist, seemingly defying solution. It may be that we are too close to the situation, and unable to evaluate all of the factors involved or possible remedies. The help of a trained, certified family counselor may or may not be required. I've often found the insights of a good friend can work wonders in offering a fresh perspective.

We've all heard the phrase, "tell it like it is." That is exactly what we need at times, even though it may hurt or make us feel uncomfortable. The book of Proverbs frequently reminds us that, even though counsel may not always seem pleasant, a wise man becomes wiser when he heeds the advice of credible observers.

> There is great strength
> in multiple strands
> working together

My sheep taught me a third lesson in mutual cooperation, although this last one came more indirectly. From time to time it became necessary to put up temporary gates while we were mending a fence or to guide the sheep into another section of pasture for whatever reason. Since we usually needed the new gates for only a short time, sometimes just a few hours, we would use twine instead of wire to fasten them.

The twine was very strong, used originally to tie up a tarpaulin or to secure hay bales. The secret to the twine's strength was that it consisted of as many as twenty individual, intertwined strands. Ecclesiastes 4:12 says, "a cord of three strands is not quickly torn apart." Since our twine had far more than three strands, we never worried about whether it would hold the temporary gate in place.

This strength did present one minor disadvantage: The twine was far too strong to break with our hands, no matter how we strained and tugged, yet sometimes we were too far from the house to get a knife or scissors. The solution to this dilemma was to separate individual strands of the twine and break them one at a time. Working together, the braids were extremely strong, but individually, they were relatively weak. By popping the strands one by one, the twine could be pulled apart.

In a sense, each strand was accountable to the others. They supported and strengthened one another, and worked together in a classic example of successful teamwork. As we separated the "team members," they became ineffective and easily broken.

Have you ever seen this principle at work in business? Sometimes we'll find a very talented employee who insists upon functioning as a "lone ranger," doing his job apart from the company team. Such a person can be very productive, but there is always a danger that he may prove to be a disruptive factor in any effort to get people to work together smoothly. Another instance would be a working environment in which morale is low; there is no effort to encourage a sense of teamwork and harmony, and employees begin working independently—sometimes in conflict. Such conditions may be a result of management policies or because the managers have not been alert for such a problem. The future for such an organization can be ominous. Once the individual employee "strands" begin to break, the strength of the company "twine" is substantially lessened.

The positive contrast to that is a situation in which the employees have a good understanding of one another's roles in the company, respect one another's talents and contributions, and can see how their respective jobs fit together to achieve a common goal. In this type of environment, productivity and job satisfaction are usually high, and prospects for the business's bottom line at the end of the year are very good.

On our farm, whenever we had to erect a new fence for our sheep, we also had a chance to see the importance of team work. I learned that fence construction is quite an art. The fence posts not only determine a fence line and hold up the woven wire, but also work together to support the barrier. The individual posts are not strong enough to withstand the weight and stresses of a tightly strung fence. Therefore, diagonal wires must be strung—crossing each other—so the pressure becomes distributed more evenly from post to post. Once a horizontal beam is fixed between the posts to keep them from sagging together, the diagonal wires are put into place. The final step is to secure the woven wire fencing into the posts, stretching it as tightly as possible, and then fastening it.

The separate elements of the fence combine to form one functioning unit to achieve a singular purpose. The whole truly does become greater than the sum of the parts. In my case, fence construction was more than learning some abstract principles about teamwork. In one respect it helped Ardie and me strengthen the foundation of our marriage.

Erecting a fence, as you can imagine, is definitely not a job for one individual. At "Johnson Acres," it was often a one-man/one-woman project. My wife and I spent many hours together building and repairing fences over the years. We are convinced the team sense that resulted from working together to get those jobs done contributed significantly to where we are in our marriage today.

> Building fences can
> help in mending
> other "fences"

I'm not suggesting that the remedy for a troubled marriage—or a struggling business—is to erect sheep fences. But in a marital relationship, I believe that if couples spent more time together, working toward mutually desired goals, there would be healthier marriages and fewer divorces. The problem is that too few couples are pulling together to build fences of any sort. Husbands and wives are busy doing their own things and, consequently, are being pulled apart.

From the day we said our wedding vows, Ardie and I pictured ourselves as partners in a lifetime venture. We have endeavored to co-labor on each aspect of our marriage and family as a team, whether that involved raising the children, handling our finances, making career decisions, serving in our church, entertaining guests, or determining where to spend our vacations.

For more than twenty-two years, like those strands of twine and the fence posts, we have supported one another and been mutually accountable. We've experienced the truth of Ecclesiastes 4:9 which says, "Two are better than one because they have a good return for their labor."

As a businessman, my association with other Christians in business has afforded a similar benefit. I have been encouraged to continue putting biblical principles into practice on the job. In addition, I am continually reminded of the importance of sharing my faith in Jesus Christ with others whenever opportunities are presented. I knew my primary purpose on the job was to serve and represent my Lord, enabling others to see His importance in my life and to realize what He could mean in theirs as well.

Even after leaving the secular business world to become a full-time staff member with CBMC, I realized the importance of being held accountable was just as great. I continue to meet monthly with a small group of men to study the Bible and to maintain financial and spiritual accountability with one another. This has been extremely helpful in keeping me focused upon those things in life that are truly important and enduring.

Dr. Howard Hendricks, a speaker, author, and faculty member of Dallas Theological Seminary, attests to the importance of personal accountability. Not long ago I attended a meeting where he stated that, even after many years of Christian work, his spiritual growth and ministry effectiveness were enhanced substantially by becoming part of an accountability group.

In that sense, sheep differ sharply from people. Sheep cannot be held accountable, yet their well-being rests entirely upon the accountability of the shepherd. From a Christian standpoint, we are ultimately accountable to God. Our Shepherd, Jesus Christ, made promises to us. Because of His nature, He voluntarily became accountable to us for their fulfillment.

The most exciting thing about this relationship is that unlike our human accountability partners, the Lord does not suffer from limited or obstructed vision. "For God sees not as man sees, for man looks at the outward appearance, but the Lord looks at the heart" (I Samuel 16:7). Another passage, Proverbs 21:2, says,

"Every man's way is right in his own eyes, but the Lord weighs the hearts."

Interestingly, I know that and believe it, but for some reason it is often easier to be accountable to another person. It is, therefore, very important to make sure that that person is committed to Christ and will remain faithful to the Word of God as he responds to me.

Let me suggest that, just for a moment, you ask yourself a few questions: To whom are you accountable? Who is close enough to you to check for troublesome "ticks," or is concerned enough about you to see that "wool" does not grow over your eyes, obscuring your sight? Do you have at least one person working in tandem with you to assist in achieving a common goal? Or are you like a fragile ball of string, consisting of a single strand, hoping desperately not to snap under great pressure?

THOUGHTS TO CONSIDER AND DISCUSS:

1. We all have been caught with the "wool over our eyes" at one time or another. What was one example in your life?

2. Do you have someone who cares enough about you to remove the wool from your eyes, if that should occur? What can you do to establish an accountability with another individual?

3. Does the thought of trusting another person for strength, assistance, or accountability make you feel threatened or uncomfortable? Why or why not? (See Galatians 6:1-2.)

CHAPTER SEVEN

IT'S HARD TO KICK WHEN YOU'RE ON YOUR KNEES

"He flees because he is a hireling, and is not concerned about the sheep."
—John 10:13—

Sometimes the helplessness of a sheep extends to the relatively simple task of eating. Lambs, like human babies, almost immediately upon birth begin searching for something to eat. A lamb, after recovering from the shock of leaving the cozy, warm womb of the ewe and entering the world, instinctively knows the best food source is its mother. In most cases the lamb easily locates the milk supply, but occasionally its desire can be thwarted by something as simple as a clump of wool.

If the ewe has not been trimmed prior to the birth, wool may obstruct the lamb's access. The hungry newborn, anxious to eat but not certain what it is looking for, may clamp onto the wool, presuming it is the food source. The baby sheep is not very choosy, and the wool is in the general vicinity of where instinct tells the newborn to go. If you have removed a wool mitten by grabbing it in your teeth and pulling, you can empathize with the lamb's dilemma. It's not very nutritional, and you can't say much for the taste either.

I tried to avoid this problem by inspecting the expectant ewe in advance and clipping away any excess wool that might frustrate the lamb's desire to eat. I never received any thanks for my concern, but part of a shepherd's job is being an unsung hero.

In rare instances, a lamb would arrive a bit short in the instinct department. The confused little sheep would seem unable to understand the relationship between his eager mouth and mom's milk glands. That can be a problem since the first few hours are critical to a lamb's development.

At such times I would take the logical course of action in getting down on my knees to provide personalized assistance for the lamb. So on my knees beside the ewe, I would guide the lamb to its mother's milk. The task simply requires taking the little head, directing it under the ewe and connecting it to the "spigot." But some of the simplest jobs are the most important. There was something humbling about kneeling to assist a tiny lamb in performing a natural function, but it was also rewarding to know I could provide such an essential service.

Then there were a few occasions when the feeding problem was not the lamb's fault. A ewe might prove to be a balky, unresponsive mother. The lamb would be urgently trying to grab hold of the milk bag, but the ewe would refuse to stand still. This could be due to maternal indifference, the ewe deciding to concentrate on eating rather than feeding, or she might be tender, making the lamb's sucking painful for her.

Again, in these situations the shepherd must spring into action. The most practical solution is to turn the ewe into a cast sheep, immobilizing her on her back. I never left a mother in that position very long, but it would give the lamb an opportunity to eat without having to chase a moving target.

The "hands-on"
approach literally helps
a leader keep in touch

As a manager in business, there were times when I had to take similar action. For instance, a new employee might need some personal coaxing (or coaching) to get off to a good start. Some employers believe in an "ivory tower" approach to management, where instructions are passed along to staff people but at least an arm's length distance from them is always maintained. That was not my philosophy. I would not do the employee's work for him, but neither did I see it as a matter of "sink or swim."

I have often heard it said that the best leader is one who will never ask anyone to do something he would not be willing to do himself. I agree with that, because that means at times the boss will have to come alongside his employees—perhaps humbly enough to get down on his knees—and help them, whether it is to provide training or to assist in completing an important job.

Another benefit of at least occasional close interaction with workers is being able to determine if they fully understand what is expected of them. Not only that, but the manager can gain a better understanding of what it takes to get a certain job or project done.

In this respect, I've found job descriptions to be extremely helpful, not only in the work place but also in the home, at church, and even in volunteer organizations. People like to know what is expected of them.

A few years ago I heard a conference speaker recount a dilemma in his company which came about because of an unclear job description. An employee had been with the company for a certain length of time, but he just was not working out. It was evident the man would have to be dismissed.

The employee was called into his boss's office. The manager felt badly about having to terminate the worker, who was a very likable individual, so he decided to ease into the matter. "How are things going for you on the job?" he asked. The employee's eyes brightened and he said, "Great!"

"Really?" his boss responded.

"Oh, yes, just terrific!" the worker replied enthusiastically.

Somewhat puzzled, the manager suggested, "Well, uh, tell me exactly what you're doing." The employee proceeded to detail the many jobs he was doing, and, in fact, he was doing them very well. The problem was, those were not the jobs he was expected to perform! It soon became evident that the problem was not one of unsatisfactory performance, but rather a case of unclear expectations. The employee never had received a clear job description; it was merely presumed he knew what he was supposed to do.

When the meeting ended, the employee was not

dismissed. In fact, he received a pay increase—accompanied by a definitive job description. The worker had been just like a newborn lamb searching for its first meal. He was willing to do whatever was required, but he could not quite find the target.

One factor in my decision to join the Christian Business Men's Committee full-time staff was the approach used by the man who "interviewed" me, Max Webb. Actually, at the time, I didn't even feel like I was being interviewed. One day Max called and asked if he could meet with me and Ardie to discuss taking a position in CBMC. I told him that we had made plans already for our annual family trip to our cabin in northern Minnesota. He asked if he and his wife, Mildred, could come up to see us. I said that would be fine. I knew it would be a long drive from their home near Kansas City, nevertheless, they came.

We thoroughly enjoyed the visit. What impressed me the most was the complete lack of formality during our time together, and Max's sincere interest in me as a person, not just as a potential employee. At no time did I ever feel like I was under inspection. Their concern was not only for me, but also for our entire family. We did discuss what my responsibilities would be, but it was Max's personal interest that convinced me that I would enjoy working for him.

Job descriptions can be helpful in the home as well. Borrowing an idea from my friend, Dr. Henry Brandt and his late wife Eva, I have occasionally referred to myself as the president of the Johnson Family Corporation and Ardie as the vice-president in charge of the home. We don't have a formal contract stating that, but we do operate under that philosophy.

I believe that since Ardie spends much more time in

our home and with our children than I do, she has a much better idea of what is needed in those areas. She frequently will discuss a problem with me, but things run much more smoothly when I delegate to her both the responsibility and the authority for everyday household operations.

In a time of
emergency, don't rely
upon a hireling

Another aspect of a shepherd's "on the knees" relationship to his sheep is presented in John 10:12–13:

He who is a hireling, and not a shepherd, who is not the owner of the sheep, beholds the wolf coming, and leaves the sheep, and flees, and the wolf snatches them and scatters them. He flees because he is a hireling, and is not concerned about the sheep.

The difference between the hireling and the shepherd is one of commitment. A shepherd who establishes a close, compassionate, and caring tie with his sheep is ready to respond in whatever way necessary to ensure his flock's welfare. This may range from helping the ewe and lamb come together for the first time to protecting the sheep from wolves and other predators.

The hireling, however, is simply that. He has been hired to do a specific job and sees no need to do anything additional. He lacks the loyal attachment of the shepherd. For instance, instead of getting down to guide the lamb to its mother's milk, the hireling is more likely to kick the lamb toward the ewe, if he does anything at all. If the lamb should figure out what it should do to eat, fine. If not, too bad. The hireling is not the guy you want to count on in a crisis. He is apt to say, "When the going gets tough, it's time to get going."

Even if someone has never read the tenth chapter of John before, its meaning can be readily understood. Parents will search long and diligently before selecting a babysitter, especially if their children are very young or they expect to be gone for a long period of time. If a problem occurs, they want someone who will respond quickly and responsibly, not someone who will panic at the onset of trouble.

Children, from the time they are born, understand the shepherd/lamb relationship even if they can't articulate it. Usually, they rely totally on Mom and Dad, trusting that they will always be there to meet their needs and to provide timely assistance. Whether it means changing a diaper, pitching in with the homework, or lending a sympathetic shoulder following the break-up of a young romance, children rightfully expect parents to be "on call" twenty-four hours a day.

In today's society, though, the predominant attitude seems to be that of the hireling. "Commitment, what's that?" many ask by words or deeds. Tragically, it is a missing commodity in many marriages, job settings, even friendships. I suppose that is why so many people take the attitude of "look out for yourself because you're all that you've got." They realize there are few people you can depend on, so put all your trust in self.

One of my great joys as a Christian is knowing that I don't have to rely fully upon myself. I have a responsibility to do the best I can, but after letting others—and myself—down so many times, I need someone who is more dependable than I am.

I suppose it's natural that we sense our greatest need to pray when things aren't going well. We may be kicking and screaming at our circumstances, but when we go to God in prayer, something supernatural occurs. When I get on my knees before God, it does something to my perspective regardless of what problems may occupy my mind. Perhaps then, more than ever, I'm reminded that I am His sheep, and need to place again my complete trust in Him, just as my sheep put their unquestioning confidence in me. There is a saying, "It's hard to kick when you're on your knees."

When Ardie was a young girl on the farm, she spent much of her time in the fields watching over the sheep, particularly the young lambs. While she was near them, the sheep generally were calm, and there were no incidents. However, while she was away from the sheep, wolves would sneak up and attack. The problem became so severe that Ardie's parents eventually discontinued raising sheep and, instead, began working with cattle. During their last year in the sheep business, more than 100 lambs were killed by wolves.

> When the shepherd
> is gone, the wolves
> are certain to prowl

Even though Ardie was a girl, when she was on duty as the shepherd, the sheep enjoyed peace and safety. When she was gone, they were in continual danger. Knowing that God, as our Shepherd, has promised, "I will never desert you, nor will I ever forsake you" (Hebrews 13:5), gives us the great assurance that even when times seem most discouraging, God is with us. He stands ever ready to give whatever help we need and to defend us against our enemies.

Many times I saw how a lamb, seeing the shepherd on his knees to offer assistance, seemed to relax, contented and reassured that he was in capable hands. I have found the converse to be true in our relationship with God. When we spend time on our knees, talking and listening to Him, we find release from the anxieties of every day.

Recently I was meditating on Philippians 4:7 in which we are promised "...the peace of God, which surpasses all comprehension...." As I studied that verse, I realized the promise is conditional upon observing the command of the verse that precedes it. That verse tells us not to be anxious, but, "...in everything by prayer and supplication with thanksgiving" to let God know our requests. I found that if I spend consistent time with my Shepherd and get to know Him intimately, I have absolute trust in His promise to guide me through all of life's anxious and trying moments.

If we ignore His presence, or do not give ourselves the opportunity to see Him work in our lives, we can expect to become distressed when life's road gets rough.

There was another time when my son, Jim, taught me a simple but important lesson in prayer. The situation was not nearly as crucial as when the ewe was struggling in labor, but it did provide another illustration of how God honors childlike faith.

One summer I was laboring with the church softball team. "Laboring" is the correct term because softball had never been my best sport. Throughout the season, my best hit had never advanced me beyond first base. Jim informed me one day that he was praying I would get a good hit, more than a single. I started the next game thinking about how trustingly he had prayed for his father's batting prowess.

During the game I batted several times, but there was no indication that the object was to advance beyond first base. On my final time to home plate, I looked out of the corner of my eye toward the stands and saw my son watching intently. "Lord," I prayed, "I sure don't want to disappoint Jim."

To my surprise—and probably to everyone else's—I made solid contact with the ball, and it soared into the outfield. Although I hadn't done it all season, I rounded first base as gracefully as I could and steamed into second. I had a double! Not only that, but the hit also drove in our team's winning run. My hit will be ignored by the softball hall of fame, but that day I was a hero to one tow-headed little boy who saw his trusting prayers answered.

There is a lot we can learn on our knees, whether it is showing a lamb the way to his own private dairy, assisting an associate at work, encouraging a family member, or enjoying the fellowship of our loving, faithful God.

THOUGHTS TO CONSIDER AND DISCUSS:

1. Think of someone who was concerned enough to come alongside you—maybe even on his or her knees—and offer help. Who was it, and what kind of assistance was offered? (Proverbs 18:24)

2. Patience, it is said, is a virtue. How can you build—and reflect—a greater degree of patience with family members, business associates, or friends? (See Hebrews 10:36; James 1:3-4.)

3. Have you ever responded to a situation as a "hireling," fleeing when adversity appeared? How would you assess your commitment levels to your friends, your job, your family, or other activities/responsibilities?

CHAPTER EIGHT

YOU ARE WHAT YOU EAT

"I will feed them in a good pasture, and their grazing ground will be the mountain heights of Israel."
—Ezekiel 34:14—

> Once upon a pasture
> There stood a lonely ewe;
> Her stomach was looking bloated,
> She was feeling really blue.
>
> She'd eaten some alfalfa,
> She'd consumed some clover, too;
> 'Twas too late she realized, she'd
> Eaten more than she should chew.
>
> Robert Tamasy

When was the last time you gorged yourself on a good meal? Thanksgiving Day, Christmas, or maybe the last time you went to that buffet restaurant with the twenty-five different vegetables, seven kinds of meat, and sixteen desserts? Can you remember someone telling you, "If I eat one more bite, I think I'll burst"?

It's fun to indulge in such a delicious meal, but sometimes there is a price to be paid afterward—in addition to a restaurant bill. I think of that old commercial in which the obviously uncomfortable man seated at the dinner table kept repeating, "I can't believe I ate the whole thing!" In the background, his unsympathetic wife assures him, "You ate it, Ralph!"

People are not the only ones to suffer from such maladies. Sheep can be equally guilty of overeating, especially when they are let loose to graze in some lush pasture. The consequences for them can be disastrous. We humans know that, "You can get too much of a good thing," and, "It's not good to do anything to excess," but sheep either have never heard of such warnings or simply pay no attention to them.

Legumes such as leafy alfalfa and clover, very attractive to a sheep's eye, can devastate a flock. Although pleasant to the sheep's palate, they can cause a rapid accumulation of gases in a sheep's stomach. Some varieties of alfalfa will cause a froth or foamy material to form in the abdominal cavity, preventing elimination of those gases. This bloating effect can cause the sheep's left side to bulge abnormally and force rapid, shallow respiration. Such a condition, if not promptly treated, can result in more than simple discomfort. In extreme cases, the sheep's stomach can become paralyzed and death may follow within a few hours.

It is again up to the shepherd to be alert to this potential hazard for his flock. If he spots a pasture that could be so inviting that his sheep eat themselves to death, he can take precautionary measures by first feeding them dry hay. This coarse feed helps to stimulate a sheep's belching mechanism and keeps the ingested greens from forming into a health-threatening mass in the stomach.

If a sheep does become bloated, there are various preparations available for treating the ailment as well as time-honored remedies ranging from massaging the animal's abdomen to having a veterinarian puncture the stomach in emergency cases to allow the gases and froth to escape.

A key to successful
living is giving up
the right to bloat

Fortunately, I've never eaten so much that I needed my stomach punctured, but I have overdone myself in some other areas. We can all recall times when we did things like being exposed to too much sun, over-working, exercising to excess, wasting too much time, or even spending too much money on a shopping trip. When sheep become bloated, the problem is usually traced to their diet. Humans, however, can become bloated on a variety of things.

In a Christian context, I believe it is possible to become spiritually bloated. Now, more than at any other time in history, we have the advantage of indulging in a bountiful smorgasbord of Christian teaching. We have thousands of books and tapes on all areas of Christian living, films, seminars, conferences, retreats, Christian television shows (even a national Christian network), toys, games, and crafts. This does not even count the activities available through our own churches. Incredibly, despite this abundance, experts report the impact of the gospel upon our society appears to be comparatively minor.

Could it be that we are feeding, feeding, and feeding, but not using what we take in? The Bible calls for us to be wise stewards, and I believe that includes the stewardship of spiritual understanding God gives to us. That means we need to learn how to apply our biblical knowledge in practical, everyday ways. For a shepherd, a bloated sheep is not an uncommon sight. I wonder, as Christ looks at His church, if He does not find bloating common there, too?

Sheep can encounter other digestive dangers besides lush pastures. Like crawling infants and toddlers, sheep are not very particular about what they put into their mouths. This is another cause for constant vigilance by the shepherd.

I'm reminded of another TV commercial which has been running for a number of years. In it, two boys are debating who should be the first to try a new brand of cereal. Finally, they decide, "I know! We'll get Mikey to try it. He'll eat anything." And he did. For the shepherd, raising sheep is like overseeing a whole flock of Mikeys. If the sheep can't have rich, green food, they'll settle for weeds of all shapes and varieties—or virtually anything else they can reasonably chew and swallow.

Times when sheep are getting just the right mixture of feed can cause a shepherd to relax his guard. He must remind himself constantly that some poisonous weed could jeopardize his entire flock. A wise shepherd will inspect a new pasture before allowing his sheep to graze. It is always best to weed out potential problems before they occur.

We had a pond on our farm. The sheep were fond of congregating around it as they grazed. We kept a close watch on them, however, because there always seemed to be some new variety of vegetation appearing around the water's edge. One summer a weed containing copper began growing there. Before we could remove the plants, several sheep ate some and became sick. Two of the animals died.

Other than removing either the sheep or the noxious plants, there was one other way of trying to keep the sheep on an acceptable diet. If sheep are provided enough good pasture land, generally, they will not bother with lesser quality plants. They eat weeds only if nothing better is available.

The point is not to teach you all about how sheep eat, although I do think their feeding habits can teach us a number of valuable lessons. Among the most obvious would pertain to our own dietary intake. Charlie "Tremendous" Jones, the motivational speaker and author, is a good friend of mine. He says any person will be the same five years from now as he is today except for the people he meets and the books he reads. My apologies to Charlie, but Ardie adds one additional category to that statement: The food we eat.

We are confronted daily with an unbelievable variety of edible alternatives. We can eat moderately and sensibly, selecting foods which are nutritional and healthy, low in cholesterol and sugar and high in fiber and vitamins. Or we can go to the other extreme and consume an unending assortment of junk foods, sweets, alcohol, and tobacco—all of which will ultimately have a detrimental effect upon our bodies.

As I write this, I am resolved to lose ten pounds as quickly as possible. I haven't eaten any clover or alfalfa lately, but I must admit to having a certain bloated look around my middle. I remember attending a conference at a luxurious hotel. A waiter in the restaurant commented, "These Christians may not drink or smoke, but they sure know how to eat." I sometimes think I have become too skilled at that latter trait.

Physical intake is only one aspect of our personal growth and development. It is also important what we feed our minds. Just as computers will respond only according to what has been programmed into them, our minds store the thousands of bits of information we feed into them and influence our thoughts and actions accordingly. "Garbage in, garbage out" is too true for many of us.

Just as the Bible often refers to God's people as His sheep, it also gives us guidelines about what our "food for thought" should be. In a verse we already noted (Jeremiah 3:15), God promised, "Then I will give you a shepherd after My own heart, who will feed you on knowledge and understanding." God tells us His own Word is good food for our minds. In Ezekiel 3:1 and 3:3, the Lord commanded the prophet to ". . .eat what you find; eat this scroll, and go, speak to the house of Israel," after which Ezekiel states, "Then I ate it, and it was sweet as honey in my mouth."

Jesus Christ, our Shepherd who set the ultimate example for living, said, "My food is to do the will of Him who sent Me, and to accomplish His work" (John 4:34).

Contemporary society constantly assaults our minds with an amazing assortment of messages, many of which have no godly origin. Despite that environment, the Bible calls us to feed on a very specific mental diet. Joshua 1:8 tells us, "This book of the law shall not depart from your mouth, but you shall meditate on it day and night. . . ." The man in Psalm 1 finds that ". . .his delight is in the law of the Lord, and in His law he meditates day and night." God tells us that to be of use to Him, we must have proper thought patterns. We can only control that by what we feed our minds.

Intake for today
largely affects output
for tomorrow

Even before the birth of a lamb, his life is largely determined by what he eats. . .through his mother. Early in our days with the sheep, we learned it was important for us to provide the proper food for our ewes if we expected their lambs to thrive. Sheep usually are content with hay, but six weeks before lambing time, the females would develop a strong taste for oats. It was part of the natural process in preparing for the upcoming increase in food demand.

Even with the oats, however, the ewes sometimes struggled to produce enough. milk for their hungry lambs. Soon we discovered the moms and lambs would do the best when we fed the ewes a food supplement, a special protein feed which functioned as a "milk replacer." Once on this diet, the mothers never had any more difficulty meeting their lambs' milk quotas.

The difference was remarkable. Not only were the ewes better able to provide sufficient milk, but the lambs were also healthier and grew more rapidly. At other times, when milk supplies were short, lambs would become weak and susceptible to illness. Sometimes they would not survive. In either case, they were a good example of, "you are what you eat."

Again the people parallels are numerous. We know that an expectant or nursing mother should eat a balanced diet so her baby gets the proper assortment of nutrients. In spiritual terms, we human "sheep" have the responsibility of seeing to it that our own lambs receive the proper food for their minds and spirits. I believe this means a lot more than delivering them to church once a week. We need to communicate the reality of Jesus Christ in our homes, both through prayer and devotional times and by living out our convictions before them. That influence and example will exceed and outlast anything we can imagine.

On the other hand, one of the greatest weaknesses I have observed within the Christian community is a general lack of preparedness to respond to the needs of "baby Christians," people who respond to the call of Jesus Christ as Savior and Lord. We seem to be in the business of producing converts, but not many disciples, contrary to our mandate from the Lord in Matthew 28:19-20.

A successful harvest
calls for more than
seed-scattering

I think of the parable of the sower in which one group of people are compared to seed which falls on the rocks. It springs up quickly and blossoms, but very quickly wilts and dies. Just as some of our lambs would not thrive because they received insufficient food, "babes in Christ" have an urgent need for spiritual feeding.

I've found this need often can be met best through

personal discipleship, with a man meeting with another man, a woman with another woman, to establish a friendship, study the Bible, and pray together. Through recent years I have been privileged to meet regularly with other men, sharing experiences and insights from our lives, and digging into the Bible, discovering the amazingly practical relevance of the Book which was finished nearly 2,000 years ago. Some of these friendships I still maintain today, even though in some cases we are separated by thousands of miles geographically There is a thrill in helping to shepherd needy, hungry lambs toward spiritual maturity!

In Minnesota, everyone looks forward to the coming of spring, but for farmers and part-time sheepherders like me, the change of seasons was anticipated with a special enthusiasm. Spring's arrival meant that the thick, hard, crusted layers of snow would disappear and once again the grass underneath would sprout skyward. No more need to lug feed for awhile since our four-legged lawnmowers would be kept busy chomping on eight acres of pastureland.

The first spring rain was always special, too; it seemed to signify renewal of life in the chilled upper Midwest. Recently, I was reminded of that while driving between Chattanooga and Nashville, Tennessee. The evening was warm and pleasant, and the windows of my car were down. It had just rained, bringing out the fragrance of flowers blooming along the highway. The valley through which we were traveling was filled with a delightful smell. Mentally, I was momentarily transported back to Minnesota and the gentle, trusting sheep.

It is interesting that the Bible compares our relationship with God to such a rain: "So let us know, let us press on to know the Lord. His going forth is as certain as the dawn; and He will come to us like the rain, like the spring rain watering the earth" (Hosea 6:30). What an image—being refreshed and invigorated by the presence of God, just as the spring rain nourishes and restores the earth!

THOUGHTS TO CONSIDER AND DISCUSS:

1. When was the last time you heard a sermon on gluttony? How do you think God would evaluate your personal eating habits (I Corinthians 6:19–20; Proverbs 23:2)?

2. How about the "diet" you offer to your mind? How are your present "feeding" habits affecting your intellectual nutritional needs?

3. Consider how you are feeding yourself spiritually. What steps are you taking to make sure you don't become bloated? How would you relate John 4:34 to your spiritual growth?

CHAPTER NINE

JUST A SHEAR DELIGHT

". . .Like a lamb that is led to the slaughter, and like a sheep that is silent before its shearers. . ."
—Isaiah 53:7—

Sheep shearing. It's a good way of recovering part of the investment in your sheep, but it also provides a valuable service for the flock. As you can imagine, a thick coat of wool can be very heavy and hot. Not the recommended attire for a warm summer day, even for a sheep.

There is more to the shearing, however, than just grabbing a pair of scissors and rushing out to the sheep, cutting blades flashing in the sun. Sheep shearing requires special equipment and equally special skills. Therefore, even in areas where many sheep are raised, "baaa barbers" are scarce and in high demand. Unfortunately, this means you can't be as selective about the shearer as you might like to be.

One particular morning, my sheep probably wished there had been a second choice. The only shearer

103

available had just arrived and went to work quickly. It soon became evident, though, that the fellow had been up much of the night and was enduring the lingering after effects of his liquid intake.

I was amazed at the calmness of my sheep, even though the erratic movements of the shearer sometimes resulted in more than wool being cut by the razor-sharp shears. As the man hacked away at them, the sheep had every reason to panic, yet they stood patiently. They certainly fit the description of being "silent before the shearers," as Isaiah 53:7 terms it.

The only reason I did not push the fumbling craftsman back to his truck and off our farm was that shearers are hard to find and even more difficult to schedule. There was no hope of getting another one anytime soon, so I let him continue and hoped for the best.

I winced as the man slashed away, transforming his shears into nearly lethal weapons. Blood dripped from one ewe's ear which had nearly been cut off. Others displayed lacerations on other parts of their bodies. The most serious injury was a severed tendon in another ewe's leg. Without any indication of apology, the shearer nonchalantly asked me to get him a needle and thread. He then proceeded to sew the sheep's tendon back into place as calmly as Ardie would sew a hem into a dress. To his credit, the repair work succeeded. In a short time, the injury healed and did not cause any further problems. Years ago, when someone was tricked out of money or swindled, people said the victim had been "fleeced." After watching my sheep submit to the shearer without resistance or response, that term took on new meaning for me. Have you been fleeced lately?

Throughout the ordeal, my sheep showed none of the anxiety that I was feeling. They did not even make a sound. I felt like crying. The King James Version of the Bible translates Isaiah 53:7 interestingly: "as a sheep before her shearers is dumb. . . ."

Shearing day was not always such a gruesome event. Sometimes it was funny—except for the lamb who wanted desperately to keep momma in sight. Ewe and lamb become very attached to one another from the moment of birth, and if danger is imminent, the ewe instinctively readies to protect her young one. Desiring both her affection and protection, the lamb never strays far. When I read the poem that says, "And everywhere that Mary went, the lamb was sure to go," [1] I wonder if Mary might have been the name of someone's ewe.

This intense family relationship can result in chaos at shearing time. The contrast between a sheep with a full coat of wool and the same animal freshly trimmed is incredible. It would be like taking a hippie from the 1960s, with hair below his shoulders and a full beard, and giving him a complete shave and crewcut. For the ewes, the removal of the heavy wool was a relief, but the lambs were not so appreciative. The mommas minus the thick coats temporarily confused their youngsters.

"Ba-a-a-a!", they all said, which is a lamb's way of saying, "Where is my mother?" You could almost see the anxiety on their faces, and they voiced that concern as ewes and lambs beckoned to one another. Fortunately, when God created sheep, He trained senses other than eyesight to help in the identification process. Within a short time the crisis ended with parents and children reunited. The sudden quiet reflected their contentment, replacing the frantic bleating of just minutes earlier.

"Bleating" really ends only when we find the Shepherd

Over the years I have gotten to know a number of men who were separated from God, much like the lambs were from their mothers. In their own way, these men called out, seeking to find where they belonged. In some cases, they tried money and success, others attempted to find security and affection in people. Careers, power, and prestige were other alternatives. Yet, it was only when they cried out to God and surrendered to Him that their "bleating" ceased and peace came in its place.

Not long ago I was having lunch with an old friend. We had not seen each other in several years and were enjoying the opportunity to become reacquainted and catch up on what had been going on in one another's lives. My friend, Fred, had been telling me about how his business had prospered, and how he now was richer materially than he ever could have imagined. He was reflecting on the vast amount of time he had invested in his career, but also admitting some key mistakes he had made along the way.

Fred took a sip of coffee, put the cup down, and then leaned toward me. "You know, Ken," he said, "I have had a lot of success, but does it really matter?" Somewhere along the way, while pursuing the treasures the world has to offer, he had become like the church at Ephesus in Revelation 2:1-5. He had left his first love, turning his back on God and His perfect guidelines for peace and fulfillment in life. At last, Fred was recognizing his need to repent and return to the Lord.

Like a lamb bleating when it realizes it has become separated from its mother, my friend was ready to call again to his heavenly Father.

All of us, in our own way, encounter situations like this during our lives. The Bible tells us we are "not of the world" (John 17:14-16; I John 4:4). However, sometimes the visible, tangible things of the world tear our attention away from the invisible promises of eternity. Fortunately, we have the assurance that Jesus Christ never changes. In His own words He promised, "I am with you always." He never takes on a new look or develops a new perspective of life. Rather, He is "the same yesterday and today, yes and forever" (Hebrews 13:8).

Have you ever watched sheep or cows graze? They eat a little in one spot, move a few feet, eat some more there, then drink some water and lie down to rest. Then they start the process over again, eating a little here, a little there, and so on. What an existence! I think, "How glad I am that I'm not a sheep," but if we're honest with ourselves, life can assume a similar look for us.

I do a lot of traveling in big cities, and find it fascinating to observe the faces of people in transit. With the popularity of suburban living, millions of men and women spend many hours each week commuting to work and back home. Just think of it: Arise early, get ready, eat breakfast. Hop in the car, or get on a bus or train, and travel to the downtown area. Work for eight or nine hours, get back in your vehicle, and head home. Once you get home you eat dinner, read the newspaper or watch some television, and then go to bed so you can start the cycle all over again the next morning! Like my friend said, "Does it really matter?" There's not much difference between us and the sheep, unless we have a purpose that is defined by the God of eternity.

Setting a course
by the fluff of a fleece

Do you remember the account in chapter six of the book of Judges in which Gideon uses a fleece to determine whether God wanted him to go to battle for the nation of Israel? From that incident has come a practice some Christians call "laying a fleece before the Lord." In the story, Gideon, seeking divine direction, asked God to make a fleece wet with dew and the ground around it dry the following morning. Then, just to "double-check," Gideon asked that the fleece be dry and the surrounding ground be wet the next day.

If you're like me, you may have wondered why Gideon selected a fleece, rather than a bear skin, the hide of a bull, or an old piece of cloth. Although there might have been another reason, it could have been because of the uniqueness of a sheep's coat which contains lanolin, a natural water repellant. If you have ever petted a sheep, you may have noticed a slightly oily feel to the coat—that was because of the lanolin in the wool. We've all heard the saying, "Like water off a duck's back." You could say virtually the same about sheep.

It may be, then, that when Gideon asked God to put the dew on the fleece only, it would have required a specific, supernatural act in addition to the unique restriction. Then, wanting to make sure the fleece was not faulty, he reversed his request. I can almost hear Gideon saying, "You know, it never hurts to make sure!" Although I've tried it myself a few times, I believe we can overdo this business of laying fleeces before God. I'm convinced He has given us ample insight into His will in the Scriptures through godly counsel and the inner peace (or lack of it) we experience when preparing to make a major decision. Not long ago, however, I felt impressed that such a "fleece" might be helpful in deciding about relocating a man who reported to me.

Craig was ready to assume new responsibilities in a city hundreds of miles away, but only as soon as his house sold. His immediate supervisor, Jim, and I agreed, knowing the financial burden a man could face by moving before a house sells. Several of our other men had been caught in that type of circumstance, resulting in both mortgage and rental payments, and we wanted to spare Craig that type of problem. Another concern was that his teenaged son was a junior in high school. Remembering our lesson with Janelle, I knew it would be even more difficult if the young man had to change schools one year before graduation.

I planned to suggest to Jim that we set a certain deadline for the house sale. If a buyer could not be found by that time, Craig would not move until his son graduated from high school. An interim plan would be developed.

Later that day, the supervisor called me. Before I could mention my idea, Jim said, "You know, Ken, I've been thinking about our earlier discussions about Craig's situation. What do you think about setting (the date I had been considering) as the deadline for selling his house? If it doesn't sell by then, we'll have him stay where he is through the next year. What do you think?" Almost word for word, that statement was what

I had been prepared to recommend. It was God's way of confirming my own fleece. As it turned out, Craig's house did not sell by the date we had set, so we postponed his new assignment, much to his *and* his son's relief.

Again, I am not suggesting we seek to discover God's will in every matter by setting out a series of fleeces. That would mock God and reflect distrust in His ability to guide us through His Word and by the Holy Spirit. But as King Solomon wrote in the book of Ecclesiastes, "there is a time for every event under heaven" (3:1). He also wrote, "Commit your works to the Lord, and your plans will be established" (Proverbs 16:3).

THOUGHTS TO CONSIDER AND DISCUSS:

1. Some experts have expressed the view that one of our society's greatest problems today is a low level of personal commitment. Why do we find it so easy to give up when things get difficult in any area of our lives?

2. In Revelation 2:4, the church at Ephesus had "lost its first love." Be honest with yourself. What is your first love in life? What really matters to you? Why?

3. What do you think of "laying a fleece before the Lord"? How do you seek God's will for your life (Psalm 32:8)?

SOURCES

[1]"Mary Had A Little Lamb" by Sarah Josepha Hale, Boston, MA, originally published in 1830. Included in *Illustrated Treasury of Children's Literature* © 1955, Grosset & Dunlap, New York, NY.

CHAPTER TEN

SOMETIMES IT'S HARD TO SEE THE BIG PICTURE

"But Jesus said, 'Let the children alone, and do not hinder them from coming to Me; for the kingdom of heaven belongs to such as these.'"
—Matthew 19:14—

Early in this book we talked about the attraction sheep have for the "greener" grass on the other side of the fence. At times a barrier restricted their access to other areas, but occasionally they were inhibited by their own narrow perspectives.

To make the task of keeping track of our sheep easier, we divided our pastures into sections, using fences and gates to direct the flock to whichever areas we wanted them to use for grazing. Sometimes we left more than one gate open to give the sheep more freedom, allowing them to choose from several sections of the pasture. It was a simple matter to open the gate which, theoretically, would enable them to move from one area to another. Getting them to realize their freedom had been broadened was not always so easy.

From time to time, a sheep would try desperately to climb through one fence into another pasture, unaware that he could find an open gate less than twenty feet away. Rather than seek a larger opening, the sheep would concentrate on an eight-inch hole in the woven wire fence and attempt, in vain, to squeeze through it.

The sheep would butt its head against the fence, trying to widen the small opening. Its frustrated efforts would only cause it to work more feverishly. Determined not to be defeated by a fence, in its panic, the sheep could injure itself. The hopeless battle eventually would end with the sheep accidentally discovering the open gate, or when it gave up out of exhaustion and self-inflicted pain.

It would be a pointless, agonizing exercise for the sheep simply because they had too limited a perspective on the problem. They could not see the "big picture," as the saying goes. At such times I was a helpless shepherd, unable to offer assistance since the sheep could not understand my suggestions that they take an alternate route.

It's like flying in a small airplane over mountainous country. Below you, you can see a car trying to pass a truck on a curving, hilly two-lane road. It's obvious the driver of the auto is hesitant to pull around the truck, fearful of what may be approaching in the opposite direction.

From the plane, you can see clearly and know exactly when it would be safe for the car to pass. You know that if you could communicate to the driver from the plane, you could resolve his dilemma, but it's not possible. You must fly on, hoping the driver will be patient enough to wait until he reaches a point in the road where he can see far enough ahead to pass safely.

The pastor of my church shared a similar story. He and his wife were enjoying a leisurely meal in a restaurant when a bird suddenly fluttered into the room. Apparently not hungry, the bird immediately began searching for an exit. Desperate to return to the outdoors, the bird repeatedly bumped into walls, unable to find an open door or window. After several minutes the bird tumbled to the floor, bewildered and exhausted.

Fortunately for the bird, my pastor had a broader perspective on the situation. He walked over to the bird, picked it up, and carried it out the door. Then he opened his hand and let the bird go free.

Tunnel vision can
be one of the
greatest handicaps

All hindsight, people say, is "20/20." Today I can chuckle over the many times that I, just like my sheep, butted my head against artificial fences of one kind or another, oblivious that the open gate was just a short distance away. Handicapped by the inflexibility of tunnel vision, I struggled to achieve the impossible, blind to the fact that God already had provided a better solution.

I've also learned that getting older does not always make us wiser. In fact, we may become more rigid in our thinking. Sometimes a solution we had not considered has to be presented in a dramatically different way. In one specific example, a "lamb" led the way for a "sheep."

It was at a men's weekend retreat in Green Lake, Wisconsin, where 300 men and a number of their sons had assembled. This event featured an abundance of good Christian fellowship, but its emphasis was on evangelism. The weekend was filled with discussion of the Bible, singing hymns, and men talking openly and unashamedly about their lives. It was evident that God was touching the hearts of many of the men present—even the non-Christians.

On Sunday morning, as the retreat was coming to a close, a time was set aside for men to tell what the weekend had meant to them. Several expressed how inspiring the time had been. Most moving, however, were the brief testimonies of new Christians who had surrendered their lives to Jesus Christ during the last 48 hours.

One young man walked to the microphone and explained that he and his family had been praying many years for the salvation of his father. "He's a good man," he stated, "a real good man, but he wasn't a Christian. This morning he invited Jesus into his life!" We shared in this excitement, especially when the young man's father strode to the front of the room, embraced his son, and recounted some of the events which had recently transpired.

As wonderful as those testimonies were, they were merely setting the stage for one of the most emotional moments I have ever experienced. A young boy, probably twelve-years-old, approached the microphone and began to speak. From his physical movements and appearance, it was evident to all that he was handicapped.

"Ever since I started going to school...," he said, before breaking into tears and sobbing. Within seconds, his father was at his side, his arm around his son, helping him to regain his composure. After he had calmed down, the youngster haltingly explained that because he was handicapped, the other children at school teased him and made fun of him. "But I know...Jesus loves me...," he announced, "and I just...wanted you to know that He loves you, too!"

His simple statement finished, the boy returned to his seat. While he had been standing at the front, an incredible hush had fallen over the hundreds of men in the room. As he sat down, however, the room exploded into applause as everyone saluted the young man's courage and the source of his strength, Jesus Christ.

Within moments, a burly man in his 40s walked quickly to the microphone. "Just now, because of that young fellow—I don't even know where he is sitting—and what he said, I am giving my heart to Jesus Christ," he declared, a broad smile bursting across his face. While he was going back to his own seat, the man spotted the boy, walked over to him, and gave him a huge hug.

Unfortunately, words are inadequate to capture the thrill of that moment. As I looked around, there was hardly a dry eye in the room. Some men wept openly, they were so moved.

Perhaps, until that time, the man may have resisted the call of Christ due to worldly concerns or pride. He had believed that his was a better way. Yet, through the simple words of a young boy, he finally came to the realization of how restricted his own perspective had been. The uncomplicated, uncluttered hope of Jesus Christ had been communicated, and at last the man found the gate to a better pasture. ". . .And a little boy will lead them" (Isaiah 11:6).

Wise sheep don't go wagging their tails behind them

In caring for sheep, there is another example of the need to gain a broader understanding of many situations. Have you ever seen sheep—or pictures of sheep—with long tails? You probably haven't, but sheep are born with long tails similar to that of a dog, except the tail is covered with wool.

From an appearance standpoint, sheep look better with short tails, but short tails also are better from the perspective of cleanliness. If left on, the long tails would collect waste materials which, in turn, would attract flies, so they need to be removed. The process is not extremely painful, but it does cause some discomfort and even brief disorientation.

When we first got our sheep, we had to cut the tails off with a knife and cauterize the wound. In the last years, we used rubberized O-rings that cut off blood circulation to the tails, eventually causing them to fall off without harm to the sheep. For several hours after the O-ring was applied, a sheep would lose its equilibrium and experience difficulty when walking. After a while, the lamb's balance would return. About ten days later its tail would drop off, much like the placenta falls off a newborn baby.

From a shortsighted viewpoint, it seemed unfortunate to cause the pain, even though it did not last long. For the sheep's long-term well-being, however, it was the most humane thing to do. It was far better than the assorted ailments that were certain to result from a long, dirty tail.

In 1972, I encountered a similar lesson in a drastically different geographic setting. My family and I had the opportunity to travel to Columbia, South America, where I had volunteered to assist with the installation of a telephone system for a jungle base camp established by the Wycliffe Bible Translators missionary organization. The base camp was a two-or three-square-mile village situated just at the edge of a dense, tropical jungle. From there, Wycliffe support personnel were sent out to work with primitive native tribes, not only in Colombia but also in other adjoining South American countries.

Soon after we arrived at the base camp, I noticed that the Colombian nationals made extensive use of machetes—large, heavy cutting tools with broad blades which looked like oversized butcher knives. In a way, these machetes were like the kitchen devices which cut, slice, dice, chop, and do who knows what else. The Colombians could wield their machetes with great skill, using them to chop wood, cut grass, butcher pigs, even to kill snakes.

During the first few days of our stay at the base camp, I frequently wondered, "Why don't these guys use axes instead of those heavy knives?" Having used an ax for some of those same tasks at home, I figured the Colombians were simply unenlightened. However, it took several months to get the phone system set up and operable, so I had many occasions to watch the machetes in action. It was amazing to see how skilled the men were with those knives, almost as if the tools were an extension of their arms. Without a word of persuasion, I was gradually swayed to their way of thinking. Seeing the adaptability and multiple uses of the machete, I began to ask myself, "I wonder why we don't use machetes back home instead of axes?"

Seeing the "big picture" takes more than a good education

It occurred to me how quick I had been to judge the actions and customs of others, solely from my own limited frame of reference. I had failed to see the "big picture," the perspective of the people who had to work efficiently in this environment, not just for a few months but for their entire lives.

Of course, we don't have to travel to South America to find an everyday application for the "big picture" principle in business, the home, or the church. As a manager, there have been times when I had to dismiss an employee. Sometimes the decision came after agonizing deliberation and prayer, knowing that a man's livelihood and security were at stake. However, in most cases I felt the dismissal was not only best for the company but also best for the worker.

Perhaps he had proved unsuited for his responsibilities, and it would be unfair to have him remain in a position where he did not fit. In other cases, the employee may have been irresponsible and undependable, despite several warnings. Hopefully, the loss of his job would help him to realize the importance of keeping his commitment to his employer. The Bible clearly states, "If anyone will not work, neither let him eat" (II Thessalonians 3:10).

In another work situation, one of my employees failed to see the big picture. Interestingly, it also had a link to missionary work. It was after I had moved from the telephone business to the small company where we serviced welding equipment and gas regulators.

It was a regular practice for us to hire college students or children of missionaries for summer or part-time work. The jobs usually consisted of fairly simple manual assembly projects, with the part-timers working side by side with our regular employees. One time a serious conflict developed between a young man and another laborer. The young fellow was the son of missionaries who were giving up the comforts of western civilization to minister to native tribespeople in an African jungle.

Labor standards have since changed, but at the time we did allow smoking in this area of our plant since no flammable or explosive materials were being used. It happened that the missionaries' son had been assigned a workbench next to a worker who was a fairly heavy smoker. He was offended by the smoking, so the young man mounted a large fan on his workbench. The fan was positioned to blow directly toward the opposite work station, so the smoke would go in the smoker's direction. Unfortunately, the cigarette-consuming worker did not see any advantage to laboring in a continuous breeze.

Eventually, I had to mediate in the dispute. Although I do not advocate cigarette smoking and realize it can be an annoyance for non-smokers, I felt the problem was regrettable and unnecessary. It seemed ironic that this young man, whose parents had readily relinquished the comforts of home to serve a strange people in a distant land, found it too much of an imposition to temporarily endure the inconvenience of cigarette smoke. Understandably, he never earned a hearing from the co-worker to explain his Christian faith.

In my home, I've learned that discipline, as unpleasant as it often is to enforce, is part of the "big picture," too. As much as a hug or a thoughtful gift, I have discovered that discipline is an important part of demonstrating my love for my children. I need to show my affection for them, but also that I care enough to correct them. Many times it does hurt me as much as it hurts them. Proverbs 19:18 urges parents to "Discipline your son while there is hope," and Proverbs 22:6 exhorts, "Train up a child in the way he should go, even when he is old he will not depart from it." An occasional spanking or not allowing one of my children to participate in a favorite activity may cause temporary distress, but it is far better than having a wayward child who grows up with no understanding of what is right or wrong.

THOUGHTS TO CONSIDER AND DISCUSS:

1. Think of a time when you worked long and feverishly, trying to solve a problem, only to later discover you were so close to the solution you virtually tripped over it. What hindered you from finding that answer sooner?

2. Sometimes our greatest lessons come through painful experiences. How did some difficult experience in your life work toward your ultimate benefit? (Romans 8:28-29)

3. Why is it often so hard for us to exert discipline in our family or on the job? How can discipline result in positive change regarding work habits, personal behavior, or deeply felt attitudes? Consider Hebrews 12:7-11.

CHAPTER ELEVEN

TRY COUNTING SHEEP

"For you were continually straying like sheep, but now you have returned to the Shepherd and Guardian of your souls."
—I Peter 2:25—

Eagles. Majestic, soaring sovereigns of the sky. It is a wonderous sight to see these living gliders riding the wind currents so gracefully, wings spread and virtually motionless. I had always admired these special creatures until one year when we received a personal reminder that eagles are also birds of prey, ready to pounce on any small, defenseless animal.

That summer our sheep came under siege. A number of them, the lambs in particular, became victims of an unseen menace. I would return from work to find several of the animals with serious wounds on the tops of their heads. The flesh atop their heads gaped open, sometimes exposing a portion of the skull. Their ears, usually at right angles to their heads or pointed diagonally upward, drooped as the skin pulled away from the jagged incision.

The situation puzzled us. We knew of no animals in the area which could inflict such injuries upon our sheep, especially ones which concentrated an attack upon their heads. Other parts of the sheep's bodies had not been harmed, so that made it very unlikely the assailant was a dog.

One afternoon a woman who lived nearby stopped at our house. She told Ardie she was driving by when she noticed a lamb lying in the road, obviously injured. Ardie rushed to investigate and found the little animal lying still, in shock. The top of its head was gone. After carrying the lamb back to the barn, my wife put her nursing skills to work. She cleaned up the wound and sewed it up as well as she could.

Ardie told me about the incident after I came home that evening. I was surprised that the lamb had been found in the road since I knew the fence in that area of the pasture was in good repair. There was no way the animal could have worked its way through.

Our veterinarian came out and agreed that the injuries had not been caused by a dog. Studying the wounds and considering where the lamb had been found, we decided there was only one conclusion. The villains had to be eagles which had flown up from the St. Croix Valley, five miles to the east. We knew it would have required an animal of their strength to carry the lamb, which weighed between 15 and 20 pounds, over the four-foot fence.

During a one-year period we lost six lambs to the airborne attackers. It was a frustrating problem on two counts. We never actually sighted an eagle swooping down on the sheep, so there was no way to scare it off.

And, we could not keep the sheep confined to the barn indefinitely. When one of the lambs would be injured, we would try our best to care for it, but each of the animals eventually died of its wounds.

We had one other reason for concern. Our youngest daughter, Jolene, was only one-year-old at the time and no bigger than some of the lambs. We were afraid to leave her outdoors alone even for a brief time, not knowing whether an eagle might choose to descend upon her. The thought of an eagle preying on our lambs was fearful enough.

The problem eventually solved itself. When cold weather returned, the eagles stopped coming back and the remainder of our flock was spared.

Certain freedoms are necessary so we can relax enough to rest

---

In his excellent book, *A Shepherd Looks at Psalm 23,* Phillip Keller points out that a sheep will not lie down to rest until certain conditions have been met. These prerequisites, he says, include freedom from all fear, freedom from friction with other members of the flock, freedom from pests and parasites, and freedom from hunger. As you may imagine, those months were a very unsettling time for our sheep. Generally, a fence offers enough security for a sheep, but the terror from the air kept them anxious and restless that entire summer.

Even though the lambs seemed to be the primary target for the eagles due to their size, the ewes remained tense, sensing their inability to defend against the sudden invasions. The sheep's helplessness never was more evident than during those harrowing months.

Interestingly, the Bible, in offering the assurance that God will provide His strength for us in times of need, uses eagles as an illustration: "Yet those who wait for the Lord will gain new strength; they will mount up with wings like eagles..." (Isaiah 40:31).

I suspect we all have experienced times of anxiety, when it seemed someone or something was about to pounce and bring harm to us. As I trust in God and His ever watchful protection, I find great comfort in the knowledge that an enemy cannot come upon me unseen.

Not long before we were to bid farewell to life in Minnesota and move to the rolling hills and warmer temperatures of southeastern Tennessee, I became friends with a policeman named Greg. His wife had become a Christian and had joined our church. Greg, although not a Christian and, in fact, somewhat skeptical of his wife's faith, occasionally came to church with her.

After I had known him for awhile, I invited him to attend a Christian Business Men's Committee luncheon. During the luncheon, a businessman explained how he had made a decision for Jesus Christ, and at the close of the meeting, Greg marked one of the registration cards indicating that he had prayed to ask Christ into his life. When I learned of my new friend's response, I wanted to get together with him to discuss it. Ordinarily, if he had been a businessman I would have stopped by his office or invited him to lunch, but a policeman's "office" is his patrol car, which made my plans to follow up on him more difficult to carry out.

I had talked with Greg by phone, but wanted to wait

until I saw him face to face to discuss such a sensitive subject. Finally, I thought maybe I could ride along with him in his police car for part of a day. That would give us plenty of time for a meaningful spiritual discussion. Greg said he was eager to talk with me, too, but first had to get clearance from his supervisor before I could ride in the car with him.

One morning about 10:30 he called, excited to tell me that he had finally received the approval from his captain. "That's great, Greg," I replied, "but I'm going out of town in about two hours. I'll be gone for ten days, and I've got a meeting to go to before I leave." Although he said he understood, I could tell by the tone of Greg's voice that he was disappointed.

My meeting was in the St. Paul suburb of Maplewood, at the international headquarters of the 3M Corporation. I went to the meeting, and it ended promptly at noon. I hurried to my car, confident that I had enough time to go home, pick up Ardie, and drive to the airport. As I pulled on the roadway from the 3M parking lot, my car hesitated and then stopped abruptly. I had run out of gas. Discussing this incident afterward, Ardie commented she can't ever remember me running out of gas before, and I never have since. But this one time, without question, my car was out of fuel.

I let the car's momentum take it through the intersection, and then it came to a halt, blocking one traffic lane. "Oh, great," I thought, wondering where I could get some gas, knowing I might miss my flight, and concerned about my car impeding traffic flow on a busy highway. It was then that I noticed two patrol cars parked in a lot not far away. My first thought was that I might get a ticket for obstructing traffic, but I walked toward the cars, hoping the officers could assist me.

As I neared the cars, I could hardly believe it, but one of the policemen was my friend, Greg. Immediately, he came to my aid. He had the other patrolman pull his cruiser behind mine with the emergency lights on, and Greg rushed me to the nearest service station several miles away. To avoid any delay, he commanded the station attendant to give me a can of gasoline, and we were quickly headed back to my car.

During the course of our brief ride together, Greg poured out his heart to me about some difficult things he was facing in his life. I could tell how important it was for him to talk with someone he felt was interested and understanding. I thought about how, just 90 minutes before, I had told Greg I would not be able to meet with him for at least ten days! It was evident that God had a different plan, and that my running out of gas was certainly no accident.

After I returned from my trip, Greg and I began meeting once a week and had enough time together for him to discover many of the beautiful promises God gives to us in the Bible. Before my family and I moved to Chattanooga, Greg had gained clear assurance that Jesus Christ is his personal Savior and Lord. Even though primarily by long distance, we keep in contact and have maintained our friendship centered upon Christ.

It is fun to anticipate
new experiences
to replace the old

At last the time came for us to part with our sheep. We

had enjoyed having them and had learned countless lessons from them, but we were ready to move to a new home and to new things. As we sold the last of the sheep, we realized they had not netted us a monetary fortune, but the experiences had been invaluable for all of us.

I prepared to load the sheep into my truck and drive them to the stockyards in South St. Paul. I had made the trip numerous times, backing the truck up to one of the ramps at a huge livestock center. As I dropped the tailgate of my truck, the sheep, one after another, would venture out and walk down a narrow wooden walkway to a pen. I would be given a receipt and drive away, knowing a check for the sheep would arrive in a few days.

Once in awhile, one of the sheep would manage to sneak out of the building before the door closed and romp across the paved lot surrounding the stockyard buildings. Knowing how elusive those animals can be, I would smile and think to myself, "I'm sure glad I'm not responsible for catching that sheep."

The day we officially sold the remainder of our sheep remains vividly impressed upon my mind. As it happened, Bob Tamasy was in town that evening on CBMC business and stayed in our home. I invited him to ride along for the grand finale, although we did not realize at the time we would collaborate one day on a book about my woolly friends.

One final time that evening I backed up to the large building that would temporarily house the sheep. As I opened the rear gate of the truck, the sheep hesitated briefly as they often did. However, once one of them stepped out and headed down the ramp, the others dutifully followed. There were no goodbyes. To be honest, I shed no tears and had no regrets. It had been a good fourteen years with the sheep, but as King Solomon wrote, "To everything there is a season, and a time to every purpose under the heaven" (Ecclesiastes 3:1, KJV). Sheep season had come to an end.

Fortunately, life for me and my family has been deeply enriched by our lengthy association with our animals. And, thanks to them, the Bible's many references to sheep, lambs and shepherds have new, deeper—and often more personal—meaning for me.

It's important to understand ourselves as sheep needing the Shepherd

---

What about you? Do the sheep passages now make more sense to you? Can you see yourself as a sheep? How is your relationship with your Shepherd? When He calls, are you listening for His voice?

I'm reminded about a favorite story that news commentator Paul Harvey often recounts during the Christmas season. It concerns a man whose family is getting ready to attend church on Christmas Eve.

"No, I'm not going with you," he told his wife and children. "You're welcome to go if you like, but I don't see any point in it." With that he sat back in his favorite chair, picked up the newspaper, and settled in for a quiet, relaxing evening while his family was away.

The family left. Outside it was cold and snowing, so the inner warmth was especially pleasurable. A few minutes later, he heard the sound of tapping outside his house. At first he ignored the sound, assuming it was probably a branch being blown against the wall by the wind. But when the noises persisted, he decided to take a look. Going to his front door, he peered out and noticed a flock of birds flying toward the illuminated window of his house, trying in vain to get inside.

The man took pity on the shivering creatures, so he tried to think of a way to help. Behind the house was a barn. "I know," he told himself. "I'll open the door to the barn, get the birds' attention, and lead them into the barn." To his dismay, however, he could not get the birds to notice him. They were intent upon the warmth they knew they would find on the other side of the window. Although the man was offering them safety and shelter, the birds were determined to solve their problem in their own way.

"How can I get them to notice me and realize that I can help them?" the man mused aloud. "Oh, if only I could briefly become like them, to be a bird for just a little while. Then I could tell them about the shelter they would find in the barn."

At precisely that moment, the bells of the nearby church began to ring, announcing the start of the Christmas Eve service. The timing, the man realized, was no coincidence. For the first time he understood that just as he would have liked to become a bird to deliver the feathery flock from their plight, Jesus Christ, the Son of God, had become a man humbling Himself so men and women of the world could know about the one eternal answer to their problems.

In the beginning was the Word, and the Word was with God, and the Word was God . . . And the Word became flesh, and dwelt among us (John 1:1-14).

A few years ago I was in Chicago for a business management seminar. I had rented a car and was following the directions to the meeting hall. For some reason, one small but important detail in the directions had been omitted, and I spent nearly thirty minutes searching for the building.

I eventually stopped and asked for directions. To my surprise, I had driven past the location several times, but had not been aware of it. In the neighborhood all along without knowing it! I felt foolish, having overlooked the obvious.

It is my hope that this book has been both enjoyable and enlightening. Hopefully, the next time you read a Bible passage about sheep you will nod knowingly, a little wiser from this brief encounter with sheep.

Yet as I close, I would like to ask you a final question: Do you know the Shepherd, Jesus Christ, personally? If Jesus were to call His flock home today, are you certain that you would be included? Jesus said, "And all nations will be gathered before Him, and He will separate them from one another, as the shepherd separates the sheep from the goats." Have you been in the neighborhood of salvation, but overlooked the obvious: Your *personal* need of the Savior?

If you have any doubts about your relationship to the Lord, I would like to suggest that you repeat a simple prayer like this one: "Dear God, I realize that I am a sheep in need of the one true Shepherd. I have broken your laws and sincerely ask for your forgiveness. I am inviting Jesus Christ to come into my life, to lead me as my personal Shepherd. I ask you take control of my life and guide me. Amen."

Now, if you have said that prayer, let me suggest that you do not stop there. Get in touch with another Christian and tell him or her of your decision. Seek out a church, or a group such as the Christian Business

Men's Committee, that believes and upholds the Bible as the inspired Word of God. And ask God to bring another person into your life to help you grow and mature as a Christian. I can assure you that God will be faithful in filling that request.

If you already are a Christian, perhaps you can see yourself as one of those sheep that has gone astray. You have heard the Shepherd calling, but you know you have been ignoring Him, choosing to go your own way. Perhaps you have yielded to the lure of the greener grass, or you've been stubbornly trying to kick while you are on your knees. Now you sense an inner longing to return to the fold.

Jesus' love for you today is as strong as it has ever been. He is waiting for you to return. "For you were continually straying like sheep, but now you have returned to the Shepherd and Guardian of your souls " (I Peter 2:25).

Perhaps the best way to restore your relationship with your Savior is to repeat the prayer of another man who knew a lot about sheep from personal experience. In Psalm 51, King David repented of his own sin and waywardness by praying,

> *Be gracious to me, O God...according to the greatness of Thy compassion blot out my transgressions. Wash me thoroughly from my iniquity, and cleanse me from my sin.... Against Thee, Thee only, I have sinned, and done what is evil in Thy sight....Create in me a clean heart, O God, and renew a steadfast spirit within me....Restore to me the joy of Thy salvation, and sustain me with a willing spirit.*

THOUGHTS TO CONSIDER AND DISCUSS:

1. It can be tremendously frustrating to have all the pieces of our lives seemingly in order, only to have the unexpected turn it into turmoil. What are your fears or anxieties concerning your career, your marriage, your family, or your future in general?

2. Sometimes God will not take "No" for an answer. When was the last time you saw Him turn an apparent disaster into an opportunity (Jeremiah 29:11)?

3. Throughout this book, a number of illustrations about sheep have been given, showing many ways in which they are similar to people. Which example has been most meaningful to you? Why?

4. In what ways do you depend upon the Shepherd? How would you compare your role as a "sheep" to Christ's position as your Shepherd? Consider Jeremiah 33:3.